COMMUNITY SPIRIT

AUTHORS

ELAINE MEI AOKI • VIRGINIA ARNOLD • JAMES FLOOD • JAMES V. HOFFMAN • DIANE LAPP

MIRIAM MARTINEZ • ANNEMARIE SULLIVAN PALINCSAR • MICHAEL PRIESTLEY • CARL B. SMITH

WILLIAM H. TEALE • JOSEFINA VILLAMIL TINAJERO • ARNOLD W. WEBB • KAREN D. WOOD

Macmillan McGraw-Hill

NEW YORK • FARMINGTON

Authors, Consultants, and Reviewers

MULTICULTURAL AND EDUCATIONAL
CONSULTANTS

Alma Flor Ada, Yvonne Beamer, Joyce Buckner,
Helen Gillotte, Cheryl Hudson, Narcita Medina,
Lorraine Monroe, James R. Murphy, Sylvia Peña,
Joseph B. Rubin, Ramon Santiago, Cliff Trafzer,
Hai Tran, Esther Lee Yao

LITERATURE CONSULTANTS

Ashley Bryan, Joan I. Glazer, Paul Janeczko,
Margaret H. Lippert

INTERNATIONAL CONSULTANTS

Edward B. Adams, Barbara Johnson,
Raymond L. Marshall

MUSIC AND AUDIO CONSULTANTS

John Farrell, Marilyn C. Davidson,
Vincent Lawrence, Sarah Pirtle, Susan R. Synder,
Rick and Deborah Witkowski, Eastern Sky Media
Services, Inc.

TEACHER REVIEWERS

Terry Baker, Jane Bauer, James Bedi, Nora Bickel,
Vernell Bowen, Donald Cason, Jean Chaney,
Carolyn Clark, Alan Cox, Kathryn DesCarpentrie,
Carol L. Ellis, Roberta Gale, Brenda Huffman,
Erma Inscore, Sharon Kidwell, Elizabeth Love,
Isabel Marcus, Elaine McCraney, Michelle Moraros,
Earlene Parr, Dr. Richard Potts, Jeanette Pulliam,
Michael Rubin, Henrietta Sakamaki,
Kathleen Cultron Sanders, Belinda Snow,
Dr. Jayne Steubing, Margaret Mary Sulentic,
Barbara Tate, Seretta Vincent,
Willard Waite, Barbara Wilson, Veronica York

Macmillan/McGraw-Hill

A Division of The McGraw-Hill Companies

Copyright © 1997 Macmillan/McGraw-Hill,
a Division of the Educational and Professional
Publishing Group of The McGraw-Hill Companies, Inc.

All rights reserved. No part of this book may be
reproduced or transmitted in any form or
by any means, electronic or mechanical, including
photocopying, recording, or by any information
storage and retrieval system without permission in
writing from the publisher.

Macmillan/McGraw-Hill
1221 Avenue of the Americas
New York, New York 10020

Printed in the United States of America

ISBN 0-02-181132-6 / 3, L.9, U.1

1 2 3 4 5 6 7 8 9 CJK 02 01 00 99 98 97

Community Spirit

Contents

A Fruit & Vegetable Man

by Roni Schotter
illustrated by Jeanette Winter

13

Ruby Rubenstein was a fruit and vegetable man. His motto was "I take care." Six mornings a week, long before the sun was up, Ruby was.

"Is it time, Ruby?" his wife Trudy always asked from deep under the covers.

"It's time," Ruby always answered. Then he'd jump out of bed, touch his knees, then his toes, and hurry uptown to market to choose the ripest fruit and vegetables for his store.

For nearly fifty years it had been so—ever since he and Trudy first sailed across the ocean to make a new life together.

Every morning before school, Sun Ho and his sister,
Young Mee, who with their family, had just flown across
the sky to make a new life together, came to watch Ruby
work his magic.

"Yo-ho, Mr. Ruby!" Sun Ho would call out. "Show me!"

And nodding to Sun Ho, Ruby would pile apples, tangerines, and pears in perfect pyramids, arrange grapes in diamonds, insert a head of lettuce as accent, then tuck in a bunch of broccoli or a bit of watercress for trim.

It was like seeing a great artist at work. Sun Ho felt honored to be there. "Like a painting, Mr. Ruby!" he would say shyly.

Ruby always smiled, and his smile filled Sun Ho with happiness and, deep inside, a strange feeling that was like wishing. Sun Ho watched as Ruby juggled cantaloupes, then cut them into wedges and packed them neatly in plastic. Inside Sun Ho, the feeling that was like wishing grew stronger.

"He's an artist, all right," Old Ella from up the block always said, pocketing an apple and a handful of prunes.

Ruby didn't mind. He'd just wink and utter one wonderful word: "Taste!" Then he'd offer whatever he had on special that day to Sun Ho, his sister, and anyone who wanted.

"What would we *do* without Ruby?" Mary Morrissey asked the crowd one gray afternoon. The people of Delano Street sighed and shook their heads at such a terrible thought.

"Mr. Ruby," Sun Ho said, "he's one of a kind."

Yes, everyone on Delano Street appreciated Ruby. But Ruby was getting old. Lately, when he got up to touch his knees and his toes, there was a stiffness Ruby pretended he didn't feel and a creaking Trudy pretended she didn't hear. And sometimes, though Ruby never would admit it, there was a wish that he could stay a little longer in bed with Trudy.

"Ruby," Trudy said to him one morning from under the covers. "Long ago you and I made a promise. We said if ever we got old, we'd sell the business and go to live in the mountains. *Is it time, Ruby?*"

"NO!!" Ruby thundered. And he leapt out of bed, did *twice* his usual number of exercises, and ran off to market.

As if to prove he was as young as ever, he worked especially hard at the store that day and made some of his most beautiful designs.

That afternoon, Sun Ho came by as Ruby was arranging potatoes in his own special way. Sun Ho watched as Ruby whirled them in the air and tossed them with such skill that they landed perfectly, one next to the other in a neat row.

"Yo-ho, Mr. Ruby!" Sun Ho said, filled with admiration. "Teach me?"

Proudly, Ruby grabbed an Idaho and two russets and taught Sun Ho how to juggle. Next he taught him how to pile grapefruits to keep them from falling. By the time Sun Ho's parents stopped by, Ruby had even taught Sun Ho how to work the register. Then he sat Sun Ho down and told him how, early every morning, he went to market to choose his fruit and vegetables.

"Take me!" Sun Ho pleaded, the feeling that was like wishing so big now he felt he might burst. "Please?"

Ruby thought for only a moment. Then he spoke. "My pleasure," he announced.

So early the next day, while Venus still sparkled in the dark morning sky, Ruby took Sun Ho to market. Sun Ho had an excellent nose, and together he and Ruby sniffed out the most fragrant fruit and sampled the choicest chicory. Then Ruby showed Sun Ho how he talked and teased and argued his way to the best prices.

All the rest of that long day, Sun Ho felt special. And Ruby? He felt, well . . . tired. Whenever Trudy was busy with a customer, Ruby leaned over and pretended to tie his

shoe, but what he did, really, was *yawn*. By afternoon,
Ruby was running out of the store every few minutes. "The
fruit!" he'd yell to Trudy. "Got to fix the fruit!" he'd say,
but once outside, what he did, really, was *sneeze*.

"To your health, Mr. Ruby," Sun Ho whispered,
sneaking him a handkerchief.

"Thank you, Mr. Sun Ho," Ruby said, quietly blowing
his nose.

That evening it began to snow on Delano Street.

It snowed all night, and by morning the street was cold
and white, the color of fresh cauliflower.

For the first time in many years, Ruby woke up feeling
sick. His face was red, his forehead hot. "No work today,"
Trudy said. "Ruby's Fruit and Vegetable is closed until
further notice." What would the people of Delano Street do
without him? Ruby wondered. But he was too sick to care.

When Sun Ho arrived at the store that day and saw
that it was closed, he was worried. Where was Ruby?

Upstairs in his bed, Ruby dozed, dreaming of spring and fresh apricots. Once, when he opened his eyes, Sun Ho was standing next to him . . . or was he?

"No worries," Sun Ho seemed to say. "I take care." Then as strangely as he had appeared, Sun Ho disappeared. Was Ruby dreaming?

For the next three days, for the first time in his life, Ruby was too sick to think or worry about his store. He stayed deep under the covers, enjoying Trudy's loving care, and more than that, her barley soup. On the morning of the fourth day, he felt well enough to worry. On the morning of the fifth day, a Saturday, there was no stopping him. "My store!" he shouted. Leaning on Trudy's arm, he put on his clothes. Then he rushed off to reopen.

What a surprise when he arrived! The store was open.
In fact, it looked as if it had never been shut. The peppers
were in pyramids, the dates in diamonds, the winter
tomatoes in triangles. Sun Ho's father was helping Old
Ella to a pound of carrots. Sun Ho's mother was at the
register. Young Mee was polishing pears. And, in the
center of it all, Sun Ho stood smiling, offering customers a
taste of something new—bean sprouts!

When they saw Ruby, everyone cheered. Ruby bowed with pleasure.

"I took care, Mr. Ruby!" Sun Ho called out proudly.

"I see," Ruby answered. "You're a fruit and vegetable man, Sun Ho, like me."

Sun Ho's face turned the color of Ruby's radishes. The feeling that was like wishing was gone now. In its place was a different feeling: pride.

"*Is it time*, Ruby?" Trudy whispered.

Ruby sighed. He thought about how much he liked Sun Ho and his family and how carefully they had kept his store. He thought about the stiffness and creaking in his knees. He thought about the mountains and about Trudy's loving care. More than that, he thought about her barley soup.

"It's time," he said finally.

Now Sun Ho is a fruit and vegetable man! Every morning, long before the sun is up, long before it's time for school, Sun Ho and his family are up, ready to hurry to market to choose the ripest fruit and vegetables for their store.

And Ruby? He's still a fruit and vegetable man . . . only now he and Trudy grow their own.

MEET
RONI SCHOTTER

One of Roni Schotter's favorite childhood memories is of visiting the public library with her mother.

"I got to choose books from a special low shelf that held all the Caldecott winners. I loved everything about those books."

Schotter never lost her love of books. She worked as a children's book editor and later began writing her own stories for children.

Her first book was *A Matter of Time.* It was made into an "ABC After School Special." The program won an Emmy, an award given for excellence in television. Her book *Hanukkah!* won the 1991 National Jewish Book Award.

MEET
JEANETTE WINTER

For Jeanette Winter, working on *A Fruit & Vegetable Man* was an enjoyable experience. She says, "I have always liked the fruit and vegetable markets in New York." Winter visited many of the old markets in that city. As she often does when working on a book, she took many photographs. She used them to get ideas for her illustrations.

Winter says, "I try to tell the story with my pictures. I also try to make the sort of pictures that I would have enjoyed looking at as a child."

From Sea to

From California and the Pacific Ocean to New York and the Atlantic Ocean, people are saying it really is up to us!

Oakland, California

Students from the Glenview and La Escuelita schools created four murals of their city. But they left one thing out—litter! Why? They wanted people to see Oakland as a beautiful, litter-free place to live.

As one student, Nathaniel Gallardo, explained, "I hope that when people see our murals, they will think that these kids know how beautiful Oakland is because of the way they painted it."

BOAT HOUSE

FAIRYLAND

Courtesy of Festival at the Lake, Oakland, California.

New York, New York

In the middle of a New York City neighborhood, old tires, rusty bedsprings, and abandoned cars once covered three lots. Then the "Lot Busters" arrived. This group of neighborhood adults and children "found" a secret garden under all the junk.

The "Lot Busters" spent six months hauling away trash and preparing the lots for planting. People didn't mind the hard work, though. As Elena Maldonado said, "When you work with family and friends, even pushing a two-ton car out of a lot can be fun."

Miss Rumphius

The Lupine Lady lives in a small house overlooking the sea. In between the rocks around her house grow blue and purple and rose-colored flowers. The Lupine Lady is little and old. But she has not always been that way. I know. She is my great-aunt, and she told me so.

Once upon a time she was a little girl named Alice, who lived in a city by the sea. From the front stoop she could see the wharves and the bristling masts of tall ships. Many years ago her grandfather had come to America on a large sailing ship.

Story and Pictures by Barbara Cooney

Now he worked in the shop at the bottom of the house, making figureheads for the prows of ships, and carving Indians out of wood to put in front of cigar stores. For Alice's grandfather was an artist. He painted pictures, too, of sailing ships and places across the sea. When he was very busy, Alice helped him put in the skies.

In the evening Alice sat on her grandfather's knee and listened to his stories of faraway places. When he had finished, Alice would say, "When I grow up, I too will go to faraway places, and when I grow old, I too will live beside the sea."

"That is all very well, little Alice," said her grandfather, "but there is a third thing you must do."

"What is that?" asked Alice.

"You must do something to make the world more beautiful," said her grandfather.

"All right," said Alice. But she did not know what that could be.

In the meantime Alice got up and washed her face and ate porridge for breakfast. She went to school and came home and did her homework.

And pretty soon she was grown up.

Then my Great-aunt Alice set out to do the three things she had told her grandfather she was going to do. She left home and went to live in another city far from the sea and the salt air. There she worked in a library, dusting books and keeping them from getting mixed up, and helping people find the ones they wanted. Some of the books told her about faraway places.

People called her Miss Rumphius now.

Sometimes she went to the conservatory in the middle of the park. When she stepped inside on a wintry day, the warm moist air wrapped itself around her, and the sweet smell of jasmine filled her nose.

"This is almost like a tropical isle," said Miss Rumphius. "But not quite."

So Miss Rumphius went to a real tropical island, where people kept cockatoos and monkeys as pets. She walked on long beaches, picking up beautiful shells. One day she met the Bapa Raja, king of a fishing village.

"You must be tired," he said. "Come into my house and rest."

So Miss Rumphius went in and met the Bapa Raja's wife. The Bapa Raja himself fetched a green coconut and cut a slice off the top so that Miss Rumphius could drink the coconut water inside. Before she left, the Bapa Raja gave her a beautiful mother-of-pearl shell on which he had painted a bird of paradise and the words, "You will always remain in my heart."

"You will always remain in mine too," said Miss Rumphius.

My great-aunt Miss Alice Rumphius climbed tall mountains where the snow never melted. She went through jungles and across deserts. She saw lions playing and kangaroos jumping. And everywhere she made friends she would never forget. Finally she came to the Land of the Lotus-Eaters, and there, getting off a camel, she hurt her back.

"What a foolish thing to do," said Miss Rumphius. "Well, I have certainly seen faraway places. Maybe it is time to find my place by the sea."

And it was, and she did.

From the porch of her new house Miss Rumphius watched the sun come up; she watched it cross the heavens and sparkle on the water; and she saw it set in glory in the evening. She started a little garden among the rocks that surrounded her house, and she planted a few flower seeds in the stony ground. Miss Rumphius was *almost* perfectly happy.

"But there is still one more thing I have to do," she said. "I have to do something to make the world more beautiful."

But what? "The world already is pretty nice," she thought, looking out over the ocean.

The next spring Miss Rumphius was not very well. Her back was bothering her again, and she had to stay in bed most of the time.

The flowers she had planted the summer before had come up and bloomed in spite of the stony ground. She could see them from her bedroom window, blue and purple and rose-colored.

"Lupines," said Miss Rumphius with satisfaction. "I have always loved lupines the best. I wish I could plant more seeds this summer so that I could have still more flowers next year."

But she was not able to.

After a hard winter spring came. Miss Rumphius was feeling much better. Now she could take walks again. One afternoon she started to go up and over the hill, where she had not been in a long time.

"I don't believe my eyes!" she cried when she got to the top. For there on the other side of the hill was

a large patch of blue and purple and rose-colored lupines!

"It was the wind," she said as she knelt in delight. "It was the wind that brought the seeds from my garden here! And the birds must have helped!"

Then Miss Rumphius had a wonderful idea!

She hurried home and got out her seed catalogues. She sent off to the very best seed house for five bushels of lupine seed.

All that summer Miss Rumphius, her pockets full of seeds, wandered over fields and headlands, sowing lupines. She scattered seeds along the highways and down the country lanes. She flung handfuls of them around the schoolhouse and back of the church. She tossed them into hollows and along stone walls.

Her back didn't hurt her any more at all.

Now some people called her That Crazy Old Lady.

The next spring there were lupines everywhere. Fields and hillsides were covered with blue and purple and rose-colored flowers. They bloomed along the highways and down the lanes. Bright patches lay around the schoolhouse and back of the

church. Down in the hollows and along the stone walls grew the beautiful flowers.

Miss Rumphius had done the third, the most difficult thing of all!

My Great-aunt Alice, Miss Rumphius, is very old now. Her hair is very white. Every year there are more and more lupines. Now they call her the Lupine Lady. Sometimes my friends stand with me outside her gate, curious to see the old, old lady who planted the fields of lupines. When she invites us in, they come slowly. They think she is the oldest woman in the world. Often she tells us stories of faraway places.

"When I grow up," I tell her, "I too will go to faraway places and come home to live by the sea."

"That is all very well, little Alice," says my aunt, "but there is a third thing you must do."

"What is that?" I ask.

"You must do something to make the world more beautiful."

"All right," I say.

But I do not know yet
what that can be.

Meet
Barbara Cooney

There really was a woman in Maine who collected lupine seeds and "flung handfuls of them around," just as in *Miss Rumphius*. The woman wasn't exactly like the character in the book, but she provided "the seed of the idea" for Barbara Cooney. The author helped the idea grow until she had a story that was like a modern fairy tale.

People often ask Barbara Cooney how she came to write or illustrate her books. This is what she said when asked about her drawings in *Chanticleer and the Fox*: "That question is a little embarrassing because the answer is so simple. I just happened to want to draw chickens." (Her "chicken" book received the Caldecott Medal.)

Barbara Cooney's illustrations always contain many wonderful details, all of which are accurate. "If I put enough in my pictures," she says, "there will be something for everyone." She received a second Caldecott Medal for *Ox-Cart Man*, and a story she both wrote and illustrated, *Island Boy*, was a Boston Globe/Horn Book Honor Book.

Valentine for Earth

Oh, it will be fine
To rocket through space
And see the reverse
Of the moon's dark face,

To travel to Saturn
Or Venus or Mars,
Or maybe discover
Some uncharted stars.

But do they have anything
Better than we?
Do you think, for instance,
They have a blue sea

For sailing and swimming?
Do the planets have hills
With raspberry thickets
Where a song sparrow fills

The summer with music?
And do they have snow
To silver the roads
Where the school buses go?

Oh, I'm all for rockets
And worlds cold or hot,
But I'm wild in love
With the planet we've got!

FRANCES FROST

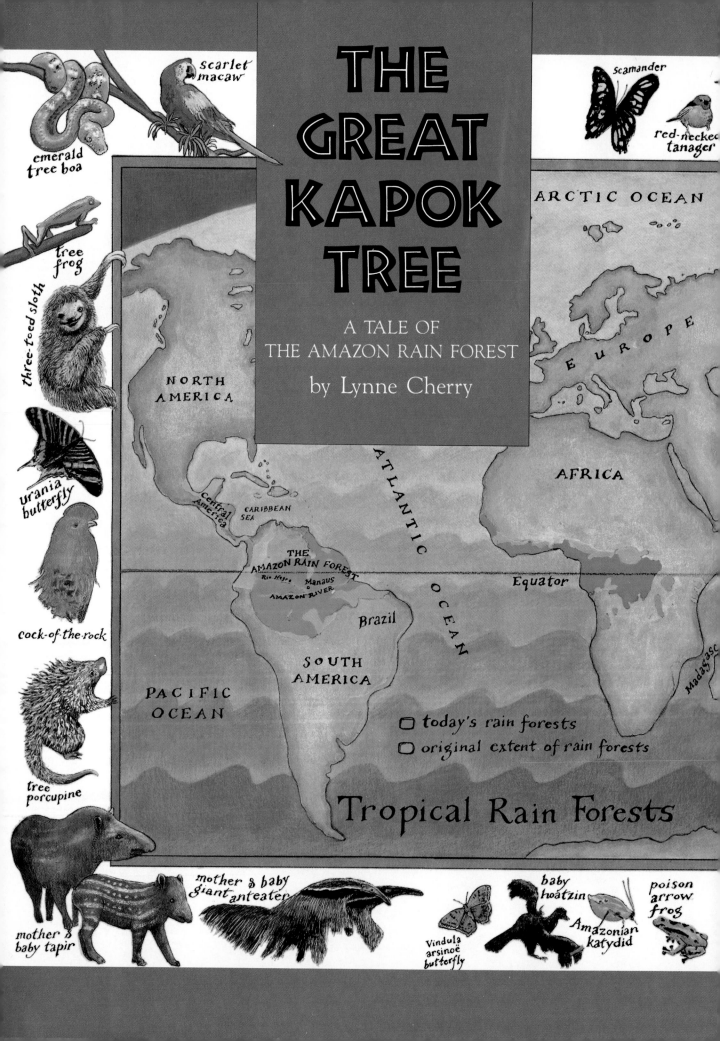

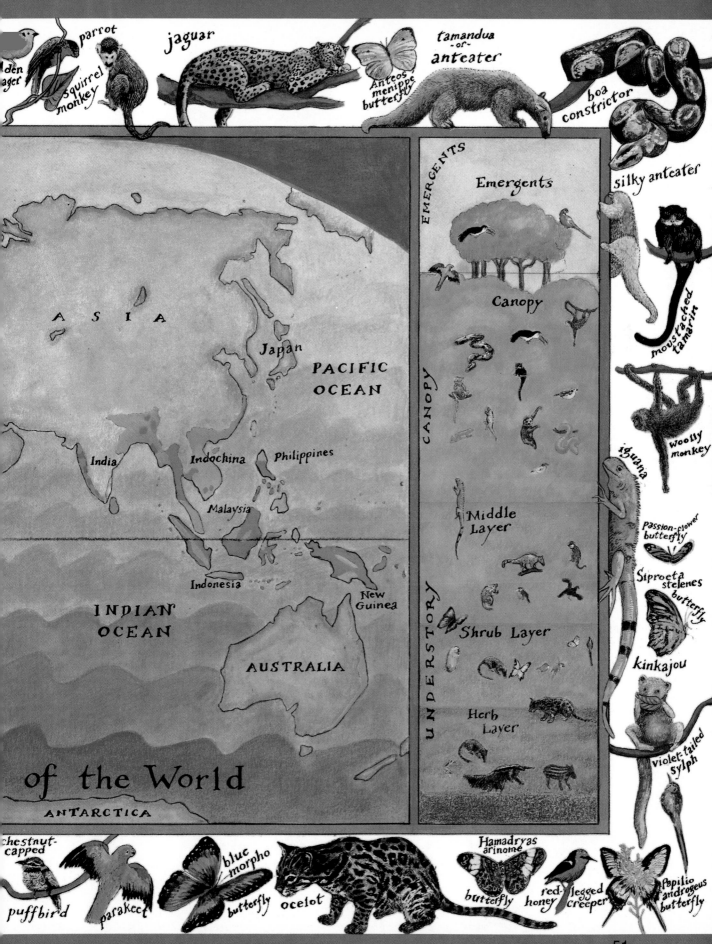

parrot

jaguar

tamandua
-or-
anteater

Anteos
menippe
butterfly

boa
constrictor

Squirrel
monkey

den
ager

silky anteater

EMERGENTS

Emergents

Canopy

moustached
tamarin

ASIA

Japan

PACIFIC
OCEAN

CANOPY

woolly
monkey

India

Indochina

Philippines

iguana

Malaysia

passion-flower
butterfly

Middle
Layer

Siproeta
stelenes
butterfly

Indonesia

New
Guinea

INDIAN
OCEAN

UNDERSTORY

Shrub Layer

kinkajou

AUSTRALIA

Herb
Layer

of the World

ANTARCTICA

violet-tailed
sylph

chestnut-
capped

blue
morpho

Hamadryas
arinome

papilio
androgeus
butterfly

puffbird

parakeet

butterfly

ocelot

butterfly

red-
honey

legged
creeper

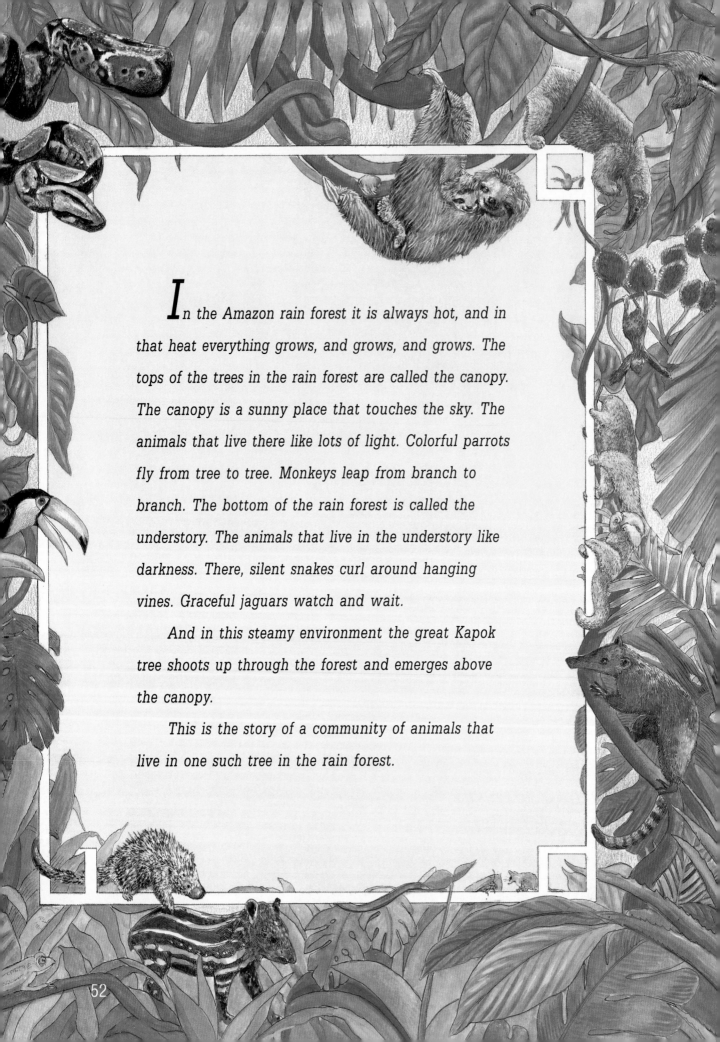

*I*n the Amazon rain forest it is always hot, and in that heat everything grows, and grows, and grows. The tops of the trees in the rain forest are called the canopy. The canopy is a sunny place that touches the sky. The animals that live there like lots of light. Colorful parrots fly from tree to tree. Monkeys leap from branch to branch. The bottom of the rain forest is called the understory. The animals that live in the understory like darkness. There, silent snakes curl around hanging vines. Graceful jaguars watch and wait.

And in this steamy environment the great Kapok tree shoots up through the forest and emerges above the canopy.

This is the story of a community of animals that live in one such tree in the rain forest.

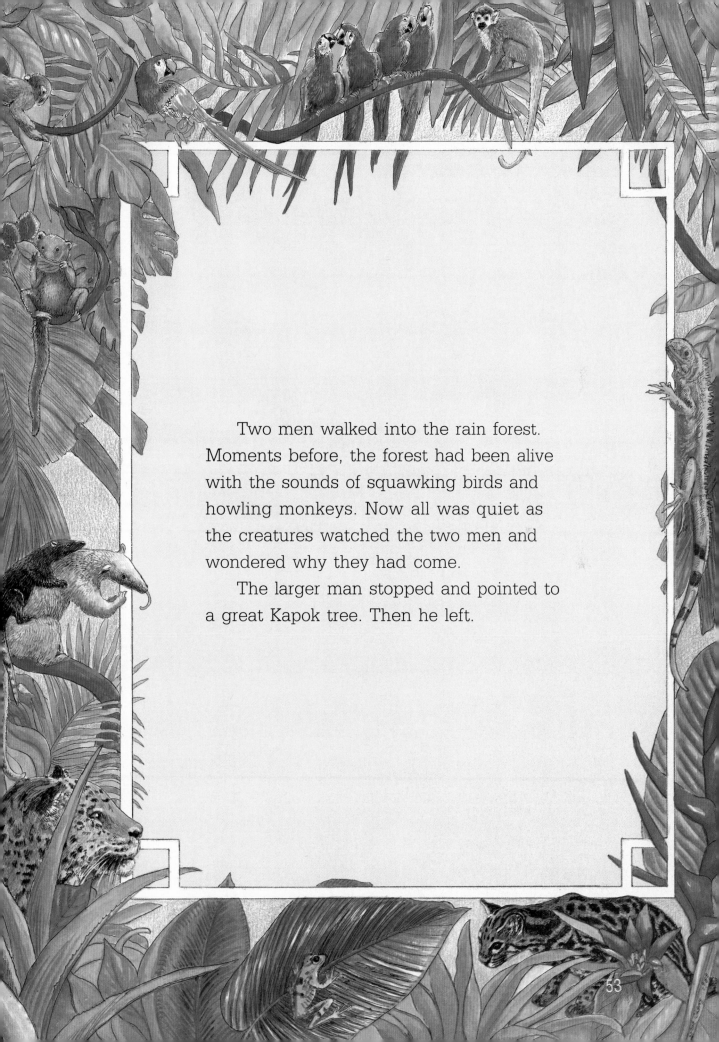

Two men walked into the rain forest. Moments before, the forest had been alive with the sounds of squawking birds and howling monkeys. Now all was quiet as the creatures watched the two men and wondered why they had come.

The larger man stopped and pointed to a great Kapok tree. Then he left.

54

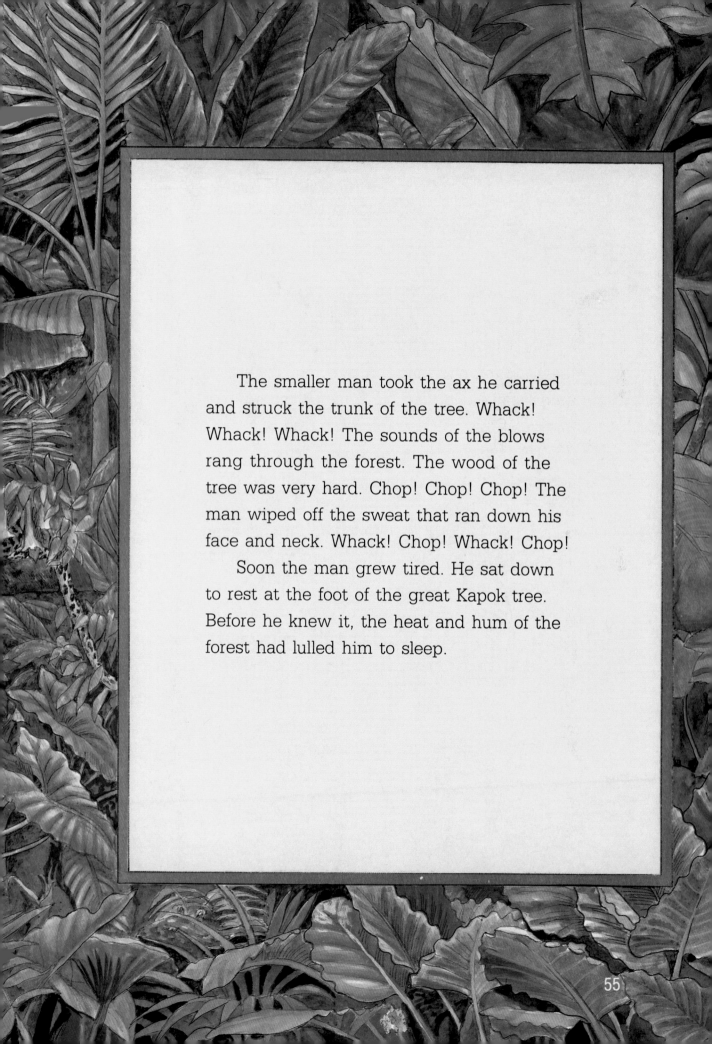

The smaller man took the ax he carried and struck the trunk of the tree. Whack! Whack! Whack! The sounds of the blows rang through the forest. The wood of the tree was very hard. Chop! Chop! Chop! The man wiped off the sweat that ran down his face and neck. Whack! Chop! Whack! Chop!

Soon the man grew tired. He sat down to rest at the foot of the great Kapok tree. Before he knew it, the heat and hum of the forest had lulled him to sleep.

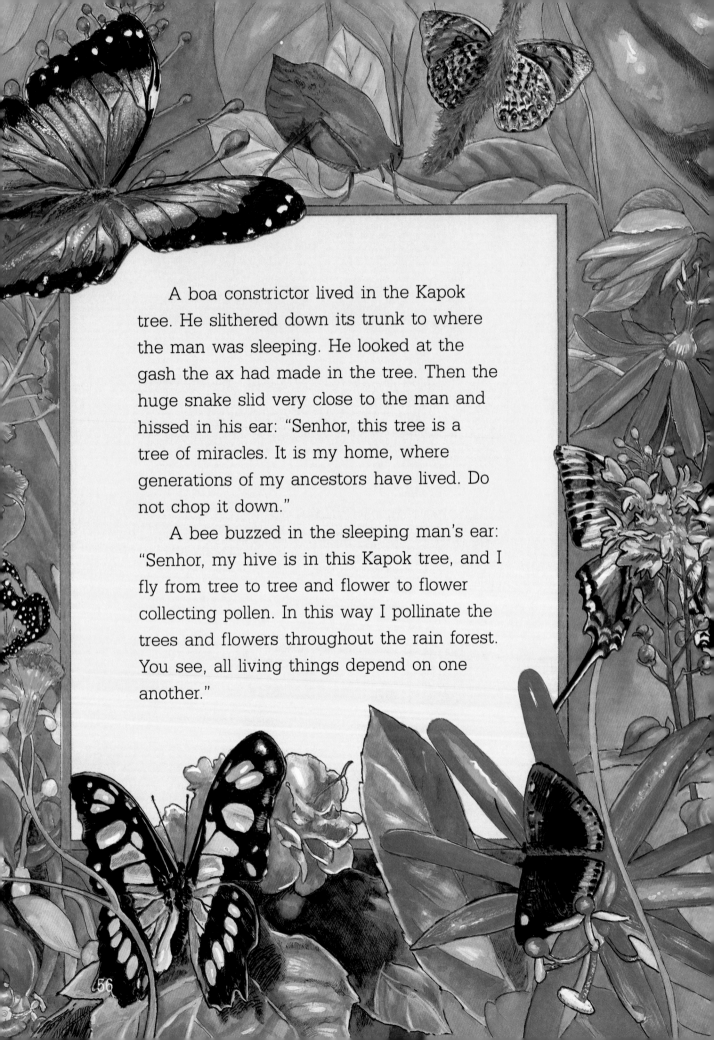

A boa constrictor lived in the Kapok tree. He slithered down its trunk to where the man was sleeping. He looked at the gash the ax had made in the tree. Then the huge snake slid very close to the man and hissed in his ear: "Senhor, this tree is a tree of miracles. It is my home, where generations of my ancestors have lived. Do not chop it down."

A bee buzzed in the sleeping man's ear: "Senhor, my hive is in this Kapok tree, and I fly from tree to tree and flower to flower collecting pollen. In this way I pollinate the trees and flowers throughout the rain forest. You see, all living things depend on one another."

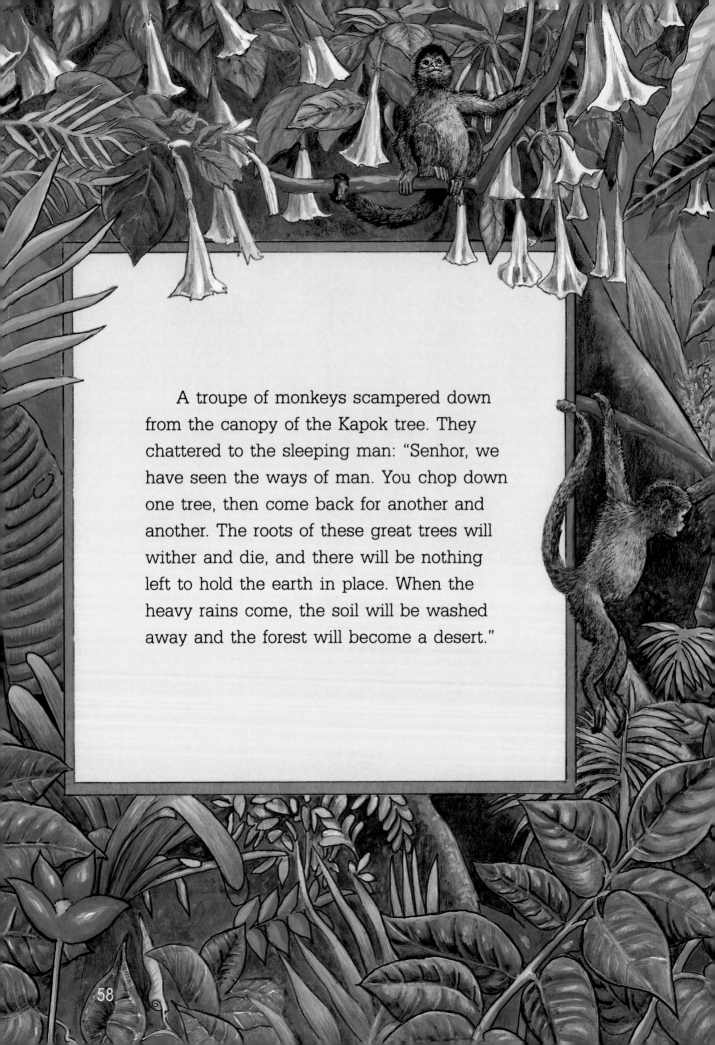

A troupe of monkeys scampered down from the canopy of the Kapok tree. They chattered to the sleeping man: "Senhor, we have seen the ways of man. You chop down one tree, then come back for another and another. The roots of these great trees will wither and die, and there will be nothing left to hold the earth in place. When the heavy rains come, the soil will be washed away and the forest will become a desert."

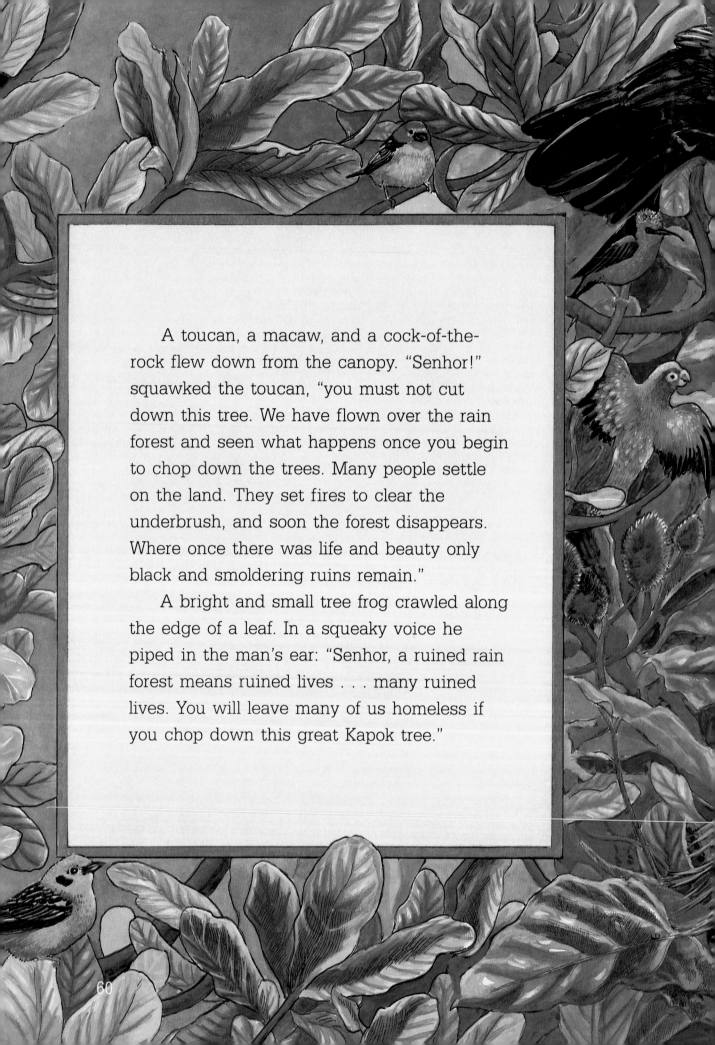

A toucan, a macaw, and a cock-of-the-rock flew down from the canopy. "Senhor!" squawked the toucan, "you must not cut down this tree. We have flown over the rain forest and seen what happens once you begin to chop down the trees. Many people settle on the land. They set fires to clear the underbrush, and soon the forest disappears. Where once there was life and beauty only black and smoldering ruins remain."

A bright and small tree frog crawled along the edge of a leaf. In a squeaky voice he piped in the man's ear: "Senhor, a ruined rain forest means ruined lives . . . many ruined lives. You will leave many of us homeless if you chop down this great Kapok tree."

A jaguar had been sleeping along a branch in the middle of the tree. Because his spotted coat blended into the dappled light and shadows of the understory, no one had noticed him. Now he leapt down and padded silently over to the sleeping man. He growled in his ear: "Senhor, the Kapok tree is home to many birds and animals. If you cut it down, where will I find my dinner?"

Four tree porcupines swung down from branch to branch and whispered to the man: "Senhor, do you know what we animals and humans need in order to live? Oxygen. And, Senhor, do you know what trees produce? Oxygen! If you cut down the forests you will destroy that which gives us all life."

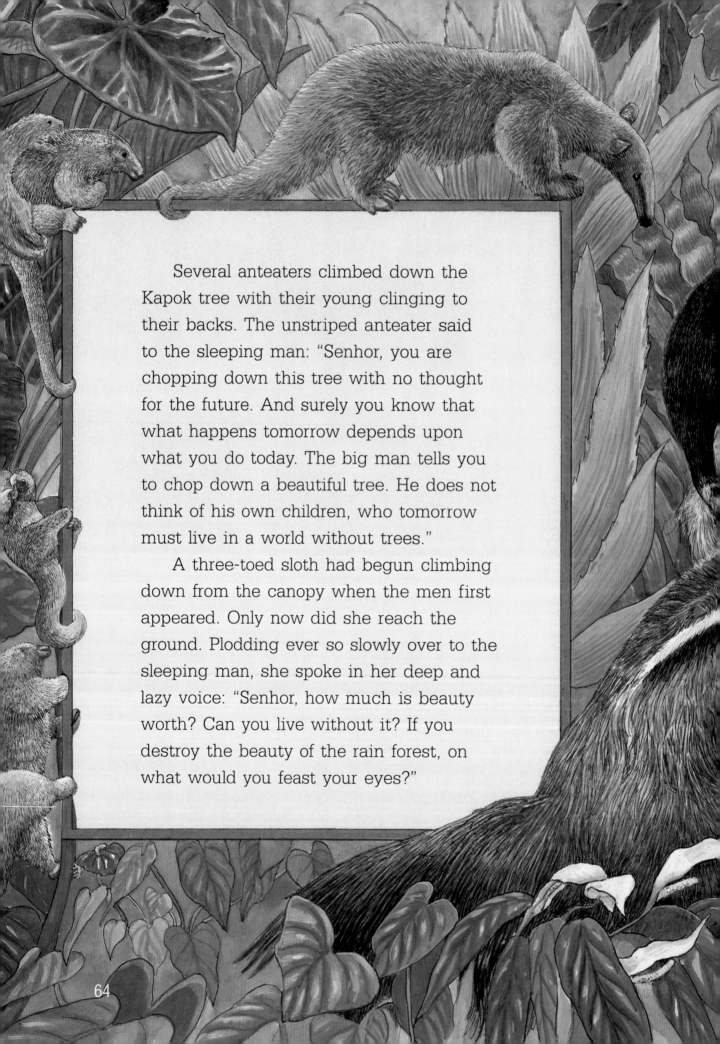

Several anteaters climbed down the Kapok tree with their young clinging to their backs. The unstriped anteater said to the sleeping man: "Senhor, you are chopping down this tree with no thought for the future. And surely you know that what happens tomorrow depends upon what you do today. The big man tells you to chop down a beautiful tree. He does not think of his own children, who tomorrow must live in a world without trees."

A three-toed sloth had begun climbing down from the canopy when the men first appeared. Only now did she reach the ground. Plodding ever so slowly over to the sleeping man, she spoke in her deep and lazy voice: "Senhor, how much is beauty worth? Can you live without it? If you destroy the beauty of the rain forest, on what would you feast your eyes?"

A child from the Yanomamo tribe who lived in the rain forest knelt over the sleeping man. He murmured in his ear: "Senhor, when you awake, please look upon us all with new eyes."

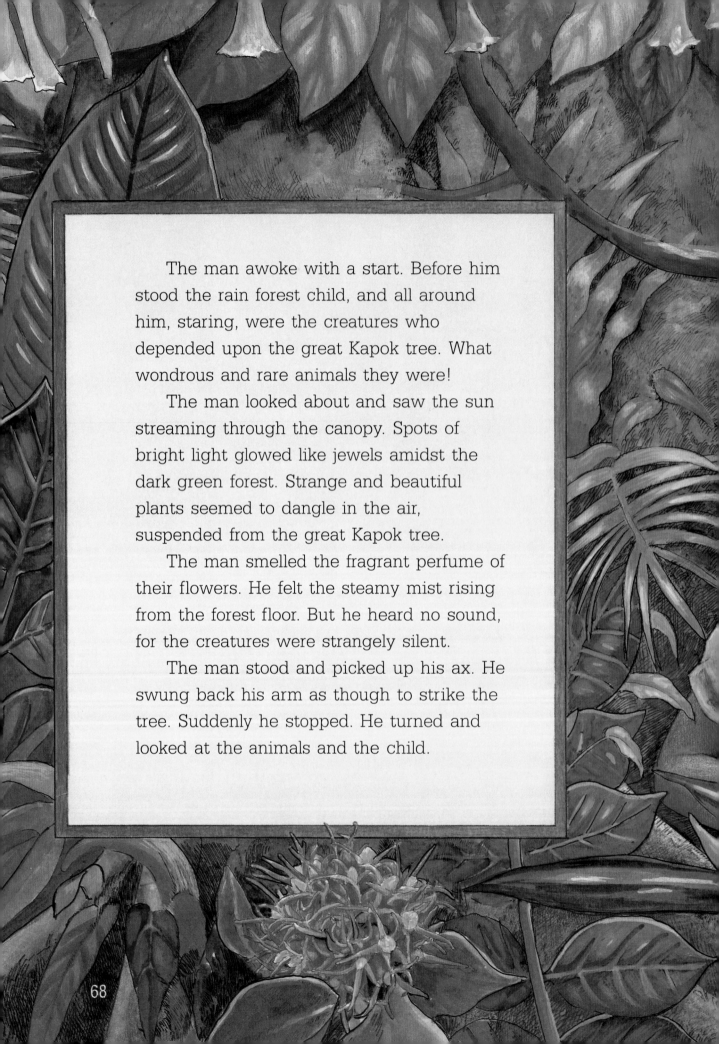

The man awoke with a start. Before him stood the rain forest child, and all around him, staring, were the creatures who depended upon the great Kapok tree. What wondrous and rare animals they were!

The man looked about and saw the sun streaming through the canopy. Spots of bright light glowed like jewels amidst the dark green forest. Strange and beautiful plants seemed to dangle in the air, suspended from the great Kapok tree.

The man smelled the fragrant perfume of their flowers. He felt the steamy mist rising from the forest floor. But he heard no sound, for the creatures were strangely silent.

The man stood and picked up his ax. He swung back his arm as though to strike the tree. Suddenly he stopped. He turned and looked at the animals and the child.

He hesitated. Then he dropped the ax
and walked out of the rain forest.

70

Meet
LYNNE CHERRY

"Keep everything that you have written," Lynne Cherry advises children who want to become writers. Her old stories and drawings probably smell like chocolate. She kept them all in a chocolate box for many years.

When she was growing up in Pennsylvania, Cherry spent time in the woods watching animals and nature. She remembers seeing the trees and fields disappear as new houses and roads appeared. These experiences helped her write *The Great Kapok Tree,* which takes place in a rain forest.

Lynne Cherry wants to "try to make the world a better place." One way she helps is by donating her artwork to groups that work to save the Earth.

Why Save the Rain Forest?

Rain Forests Around the World
by Donald Silver

North America

Atlantic Ocean

West Africa
- Covering about 64,000 square miles, this rain forest is home to colorful parrots and butterflies.
- Ninety percent of the forest that once was is now gone.

Africa

Pacific Ocean

Caribbean Sea

Mexico, Central America, and the Caribbean
- The rain forests south of the United States are disappearing rapidly.
- Many migrating birds spend winters in these rain forests.
- Scientists have begun to study how to grow Central American rain-forest plants from seeds.

South America

Atlantic Ocean

Amazon Basin
- This is the largest rain forest in the world.
- It extends over nine South American countries and covers about 2.3 million square miles.
- It is rich in plant and animal life; new species are discovered every year.
- The world's second longest river, the Amazon, flows through this rain forest.

Central Africa
- The largest rain forest in Africa is located here.
- It is mostly unexplored.
- Thousands of its plant species are found nowhere else on Earth.

Rain forests cover 3.3 million square miles of our planet. That may sound like a lot but it is only six percent of the Earth's surface. Rain forests are disappearing fast. Here is a map showing where the rain forests are located and a brief description of what makes some of them special:

Europe

Mediterranean Sea

Philippines
- Thousands of kinds of plants and many beautiful and exotic birds fill 25,000 square miles of rain forest on the Philippine islands.

Southeast Asia
Some countries here protect parts of their rain forests. Others do not, putting many plants and animals in danger of extinction.

Asia

Pacific Ocean

New Guinea
- In these 270,000 square miles of rain forest, you can see a butterfly with a ten-inch wing span.

India
- Parts of the subcontinent's 78,000 square miles of rain forest have already been turned into national parks.

Indonesia
- More than 425,000 square miles of rain forest are spread over the islands that make up Indonesia.
- The world's biggest flower, the tallest flower, and about ten thousand kinds of trees grow here.

Australia

Madagascar
- The 14,000 square-mile rain forest on this island was twice as large just fifty years ago.
- It is the place to visit to see lemurs, a chameleon the size of your thumb, and thousands of orchids.

Australia
- Only about 4,000 square miles of rain forest grow on the island continent but they are still worth saving.

73

and my heart soars

The beauty of the trees,
the softness of the air,
the fragrance of the grass,
    speaks to me.

The summit of the mountain,
the thunder of the sky,
the rhythm of the sea,
    speaks to me.

The faintness of the stars,
the freshness of the morning,
the dew drop on the flower,
    speaks to me.

The strength of fire,
the taste of salmon,
the trail of the sun,
And the life that never goes away,
    They speak to me.

And my heart soars.

Chief Dan George

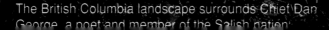
The British Columbia landscape surrounds Chief Dan
George, a poet and member of the Salish nation.

In Memory

It took a wise man to dream big,
To dream great,
To talk of peace, brotherhood, and love
When all around was hate.
It took a strong man
To stand tall,
To speak of liberty and justice
And dignity for all.
He saw a great country
With some growing still to do.
He dreamed of a better world
Where freedom could ring true.
And so today we'll gather
For a birthday celebration
For a man who sought to change the mind
And heart of a nation.
Of liberty and brotherhood and peace
Today we'll sing
As we celebrate the memory of
Martin Luther King.

Ericka Northrop

THE STREETS ARE FREE

by Kurusa

illustrated by Sandra Speidel

Not very long ago, when Carlitos's grandfather was a boy, mountain lions roamed the hills of Venezuela. One particular mountain was covered with forests and bushes, small creeks and dirt paths. Every morning the mist would reach down and touch the flowers and the butterflies.

On the hill above the town of Caracas, where Cheo, Carlitos, and Camila now live, there was just one house. It was a simple house made of mud and dried leaves from sugar cane and banana plants. In the mornings, when the family went to fetch water, they often saw lion's tracks in the soft earth. Later, they would stop by the creeks to catch sardines for dinner.

Years passed and more people came from towns and villages all over Venezuela to make their homes on the mountainside.

They built their houses of wood and the children played among the trees, in the creeks and on the open fields.

The forest began to grow towards the new village, and the village began to grow towards the forest.

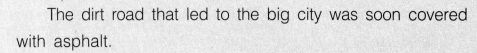

The dirt road that led to the big city was soon covered with asphalt.

And more people came.

There were so many houses that they reached right to the top of the mountain where the lion tracks used to be. The creeks became sewers. The dirt paths were littered with garbage. The mountain became a very poor town called the 'barrio' San José.

The children who used to play in the open fields could no longer play there, nor in the forest, nor in the streams.

The fields in the valleys were now filled with office towers. The whole mountain was covered with houses.

The main road became a highway. There were only a few trees and not one flower. The children had nowhere to play.

After school, Cheo, Carlitos, and Camila went to a house that was converted into a library. There they read books and played with clay and paints and board games and all kinds of interesting things. But they had nowhere to play hopscotch, or soccer, or baseball, or tag.

After they left the library, they played in the street.

One day, while they were playing leapfrog, a grocery truck came barrelling down the street. The driver shouted:

"Get out of the way! Let me through!"

"The streets are free," said the boys. But the truck was much bigger and more powerful than the children. So they walked to the top of the mountain to fly their kites. In about half an hour, every one of the kites was tangled in the hydro wires.

The children went back down the mountain to play ball. But the ball kept getting lost in people's washing and trapped on roof tops.

One woman ran out of her house when the children were trying to fetch the ball.

"Get out of here," she shouted, "or I'll hit you with my broom."

"The streets are free," said the youngest boy. But the children knew they had better leave her alone.

Dejected, they went to the library. They sat down on the steps and thought.

"There must be somewhere we can play," said Camila.

"Let's go see the mayor and tell him we need somewhere to play," suggested another.

SAN JOSÉ LIBRARY

83

"Where does he live?" asked Carlitos, the smallest boy. The children looked at each other. Nobody knew.

"Let's go to City Hall. That can't be too far away."

"But we can't go there without adults. They won't listen to us at City Hall," said Camila with big, sad eyes.

"Then let's ask our parents."

So the children went from house to house to ask their parents to go with them to City Hall. But their parents were cooking, sewing, washing, repairing, away working, in other words . . . busy.

The children returned to the library steps. They just sat there and felt very sad.

Then the librarian appeared.

"Why all the sad faces?" he asked.

The children told him.

"What do you want to tell the mayor?"

"We want a playground."

"Do you know where?"

"Yes," said Carlitos, "in an empty lot near the bottom of the mountain."

"Do you know what it should look like?"

"Well . . ."

"Why don't you come inside and discuss it?"

They talked for more than an hour. Cheo, the oldest boy, took notes on a large pad.

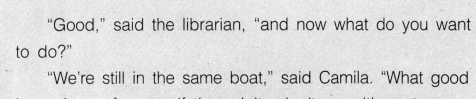

"Good," said the librarian, "and now what do you want to do?"

"We're still in the same boat," said Camila. "What good is a piece of paper if the adults don't go with us to see the mayor?"

"Won't they go with you?"

"They won't even listen to us," Camila said.

"Have you tried going alone?"

"Well, no."

"So, what do you want to do?"

The children looked at each other.

"Let's make a banner," said Cheo.

They all worked together and made a sign that said:

WE HAVE NO
WE NEED A

"Tomorrow we'll plan the details," said the librarian, and he left for the chess club.

The children put the finishing touches on their sign.

"It's perfect like this!"

They rolled up the sign and the large list with their notes.

"We're ready," they said.

Again the children looked at each other.

"Why don't we go right now?" a few children said at the same time.

With the banner and the large list of notes rolled up under their arms, the children of San José walked to City Hall.

86

WHERE TO PLAY PLAYGROUND

City Hall was even bigger than they imagined. The doorway was very high. Standing in the middle of it was a big, fat man.

"No one comes in here," he said.

"We came to ask for a playground."

"We came to see the people at City Hall. We need a playground."

"But the people at the Council don't want to see you. Go home or I'll call the police."

"Look, this is the kind of playground we want," said Carlitos, innocently, and he unrolled the paper with their notes on it.

Camila said, "We need somewhere to play," and she unrolled the banner.

"Get out of here!" shouted the fat man.

"The streets are free!" Cheo shouted back, and he sat down.

"We're not going to move until they listen to us," said another boy. "In the library they told us that City Hall is here to listen to us."

Back in San José, the mothers were worried. They couldn't find their children. Somebody said she saw them leaving the library with some big sheets of paper.

"Oh no," mumbled the librarian. "I think I know where they are."

WE HAVE NOWHERE TO PLAY
WE NEED A PLAYGROUND

The fat man in the doorway of City Hall was yelling so much his face was turning redder and redder. A crowd gathered around City Hall to see what all the fuss was about.

Then everything happened at once.

The mothers, the librarian, and the police all arrived at City Hall at the same time.

The mothers shouted, "What are you doing?"

"Take them away!" shouted the fat man to the police. "They're disturbing the peace." The policemen started pulling the children by their arms.

"Excuse me," the librarian raised one hand, "but what is going on here?"

"They won't let us talk to anyone about our playground," said Carlitos.

"The police are going to arrest them and put them in jail for their bad behaviour," said the fat man.

89

Then one mother who was even bigger and fatter than he stood in front of the children.

"Oh no, you don't," she said. "If you put a hand on these kids, you have to arrest me, too."

"And me, too," said another mother.

"And me," shouted the rest of the mothers.

Suddenly, standing in the doorway of City Hall, were the mayor, a reporter, and a municipal engineer.

"What's going on here?" the mayor asked.

"We need a playground."

"They want to arrest us."

"Those people are starting a riot."

They were all talking at once.

"Let the children speak," the librarian suggested.

"Yes, I'd like to talk to the children," said the reporter, getting out her notebook. They told her their story.

When they were finished, the mayor turned to the municipal engineer. "Is there space for them to have a playground?"

"Yes!" the children shouted together. "We know where. We can show you."

"Why don't you come and see it?" asked the librarian.

"Um—," said the engineer.

"Uhmmmmmmm—," said the mayor. "Tomorrow. Tomorrow we'll look at it. I don't have time now. I'm very busy. But tomorrow, tomorrow for sure. Ahem. Remember, we are here to serve you." Then the mayor shook hands with all the mothers.

"I knew it," said Camila.

"I would very much like to go with you," said the reporter. So the children, the mothers, the librarian, and the reporter all went to see the empty lot.

"What do you want the playground to look like?" the reporter asked. The children began to read their list. The reporter took lots of notes and wrote down everything on their sign:

We need a playground
with trees
and shrubs
and flower seeds
  swings
  an old tractor to climb on
  and sticks to dig with
A house for dolls
  a lasso to play cowboys
Lots of room for baseball,
  volleyball and soccer,
  to have races and
  fly kites,
  to play leapfrog, tag,
  kick-the-can,
blind man's bluff
  and hide and seek
  grass to roll on
  and do gymnastics
A patio to play on
  and a bench
  for our parents
  to sit and visit.

THE END

The next day, the library was empty. The children sat on the steps.

"I think," sighed Camila, "I think that nothing's going to happen."

"What if we went to City Hall again with our big brothers and sisters?" asked Carlitos.

"They'll put us in jail," Camila said.

A week passed.

One day, the librarian appeared in the doorway smiling. He was holding a newspaper with a huge headline:

THE CHILDREN OF SAN JOSÉ TAKE ON CITY HALL
They ask for special park
The mayor doesn't come through

"That's us!" said Cheo.

"We're famous!" laughed Carlitos.

"Yeah, but they're still not going to do anything," said Camila.

She was wrong. The same afternoon, the mayor, the municipal engineer and three assistants came to the barrio.

"We came to see the land for the playground. Soon we'll give it to you," they said proudly.

"Very soon," said the engineer.

"Very, very soon," smiled the mayor.

Then it happened: One morning, the assistants tied a red ribbon across the entrance to the empty lot. At twelve o'clock sharp, the mayor, dressed very elegantly and with freshly shined shoes, came and cut the ribbon with an extra-large pair of scissors.

"I get it," said Camila. "There's an election soon, isn't there? After the big ceremony, I bet nothing will happen."

This time Camila was right. Weeks passed and the engineers never came back. The empty lot that was supposed to be the playground was just collecting garbage. Little by little, the adults forgot about it. But the children didn't.

"What happened to our playground?" the children asked. The adults always gave the same answer:

"The politicians always promise but they never do anything."

Carlitos, Camila, and Cheo weren't satisfied. They sat on the edge of the mountain and looked down at the empty lot and thought about it all. Then Carlitos said:

"Why can't we have a playground anyway?"

"Are you crazy? It's very complicated."

"But if everybody helped, maybe . . ."

It was a crazy idea, but the young children started talking to their friends, who talked to their older brothers and sisters, who talked to their mothers, and the mothers talked to the fathers.

One day, Carlitos heard his uncle and some friends arguing about the playground. His uncle banged the table. He said they could easily build the playground themselves—they didn't need the council. But his friends were not so sure.

"Don't be crazy. Nobody cooperates here, not even to clean up the sidewalk! How could you get everyone to build them a playground?"

"No, buddy, everyone knows each other. They'll help," said Carlitos's uncle.

"Forget it. You'll end up building it yourself."

"Alone? No. I'll help you," said one of the men.

"I will, too."

Time passed and more and more people talked about the idea. The neighbourhood committee organized a public meeting one Saturday. About fifty people came. The discussion lasted four hours and was very loud.

"We can't do it," said some.

"We can do it," said others.

There seemed no way to agree. Carlitos's uncle and the children passionately defended the idea, but most of the parents doubted it could be done without the politicians' help. After all the shouting, there was silence. It looked like the meeting was going to end that way until one mother remembered she had some planks of wood she didn't need. One father said he was a carpenter. One girl timidly said, "In my house we have some rope to make a swing with."

Everybody became very enthusiastic and suddenly they all had suggestions.

"I want to bring some nails," insisted one grandmother.

Carlitos, Cheo, and Camila all started jumping up and down.

"It's really going to happen!"

All the neighbours began to build the playground. They brought cement and bricks and buckets and sheets of aluminum and sandbags and old tires and wooden boards of every size.

They nailed and hammered and dug holes and planted and sanded. They all worked in their spare time.

On the wire fence the children put up a sign they made themselves:

SAN JOSÉ PLAYGROUND
EVERYBODY COME AND PLAY

Meet Kurusa

Kurusa has spent over twelve years in her native Venezuela working with children in cultural and social programs. *The Streets Are Free* reflects some of her experiences with the children who use the public library in San José de La Urbina, a town on the edge of Caracas.

In her work promoting reading and children's literature in Venezuela, Kurusa has organized a bookmobile service and founded a publishing house for children's books.

The author lives in Caracas with her three children. She loves sailing and animals, and she has a sailboat with red sails on which a favorite seagull lives.

Preserven el Parque Elysian

by Mike Kellin

1. ¡Qué lin - do el par - que E - ly - sian! _____ ¡Qué

lin - do el par - que E - ly - sian! _____ ¡Qué

lin - do! (¡Qué lin - do!) ¡Qué lin - do! (¡Qué lin - do!) ¡Qué

lin - do el par - que E - ly - sian! _____

1. ¡Qué lindo el parque Elysian!
2. ¡Me gusta el parque Elysian!

3. ¡El aire es libre, amigos!
4. ¡No queremos fincas en el parque!

5. ¡Queremos el zacate verde!
6. ¡El parque es suyo y mío!
7. ¡Los niños necesitan el parque!

8. ¡Preserven el parque Elysian!
9. ¡NO PASARÁN LOS BULLDOZERS!

1. Elysian Park is beautiful!
2. Elysian Park is my kind of park!

3. The air is free, my friends!
4. We don't want building in the park!

5. We want the green grass!
6. The park is yours and mine!
7. The children need the park!

8. Save Elysian Park!
9. STOP THE BULLDOZERS!

Illustration, by José Ortega, of musicians playing instruments commonly used in South America: bongo drums, a panpipe, and a charango.

Charts and Tables

SOME OF OUR NATIONAL PARKS

THE UNITED STATES HAS 50 NATIONAL PARKS.

NAME	LOCATION	YEAR(S) ESTABLISHED	RANK IN SIZE	SPECIAL FEATURES
Badlands	South Dakota	1929–1978	25	bison, bighorn sheep, antelope, fossil animals 40 million years old
Channel Islands	California	1938–1980	24	sea lion breeding grounds, nesting sea birds, unusual plants
Everglades	Florida	1934	9	largest remaining subtropical wilderness in continental U.S.
Grand Canyon	Arizona	1908–1919	10	most spectacular part of Colorado River canyon
Great Smoky Mountains	North Carolina and Tennessee	1926–1934	17	largest mountain range in eastern U.S., magnificent forests
Kenai Fjords	Alaska	1978–1980	15	mountain goats, marine mammals, bird life, large icecap
Olympic	Washington	1909–1938	12	mountain wilderness with finest remaining rain forest of Pacific Northwest
Redwood	California	1968	34	Pacific coastline, groves of ancient redwoods, world's tallest trees
Samoa	American Samoa	1988	49	tropical rain forest
Yellowstone	Idaho, Wyoming, Montana	1872	7	geysers, hot springs, canyons waterfalls, grizzly bear, moose, bison

SOME RARE ANIMALS

NAME OF ANIMAL (KIND)	NUMBER IN WILD (ESTIMATED)	NUMBER IN ZOOS	YOUNG BORN IN ZOOS (1988)
Cougar (Florida)	30	2	0
Elephant (Asian)	X	238	1
Gorilla (mountain)	400	1	X
Leopard (snow)	1,000	292	27
Lion (Asiatic)	250	196	0
Rhinoceros (black)	3,500	130	5
Anteater	X	107	4
Bear (polar)	10,000	200	6
Jaguar	X	202	12
Panda (giant)	1,000	17	0
Condor (California)	0	68	0
Parrot (golden-shouldered)	250	22	9
Boa (Puerto Rican)	X	63	14
Crocodile (Cuban)	1,000	83	1
Frog (Goliath)	X	3	X

x= not known

Graphs

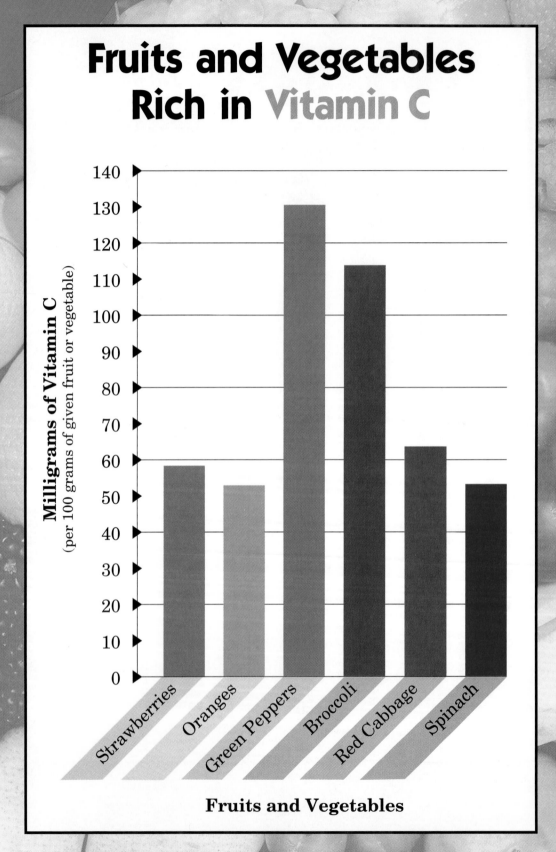

Fruits and Vegetables Rich in Vitamin C

Milligrams of Vitamin C
(per 100 grams of given fruit or vegetable)

140
130
120
110
100
90
80
70
60
50
40
30
20
10
0

Strawberries
Oranges
Green Peppers
Broccoli
Red Cabbage
Spinach

Fruits and Vegetables

GRAPHS

Area of Selected Crops Grown in the United States

CROP	🏠 = 25,000 acres
Asparagus	🏠🏠🏠🏠
Broccoli	🏠🏠🏠🏠🏠
Carrots	🏠🏠🏠🏠
Honeydew Melons	🏠
Lettuce	🏠🏠🏠🏠🏠🏠🏠🏠🏠
Strawberries	🏠🏠
Sweet Potatoes	🏠🏠🏠
Tomatoes	🏠🏠🏠🏠🏠🏠🏠🏠🏠🏠🏠🏠🏠🏠🏠🏠🏠

Citrus Fruit Eaten in the United States (per year)

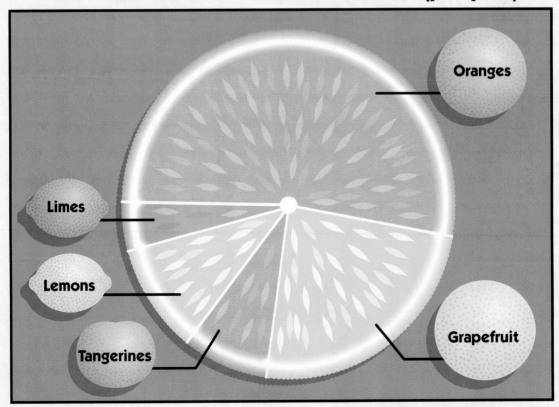

Maps

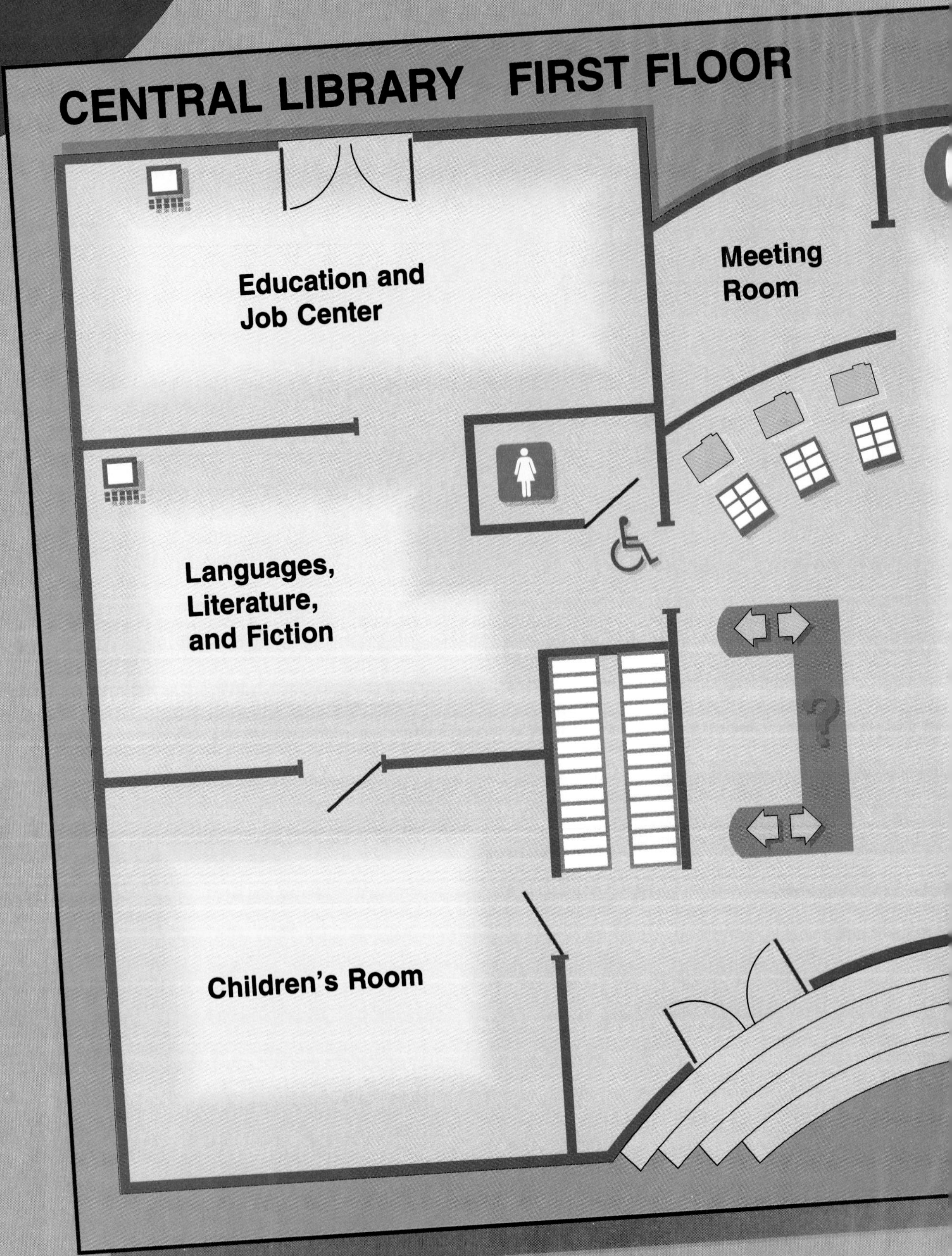

CENTRAL LIBRARY   FIRST FLOOR

Education and
Job Center

Meeting
Room

Languages,
Literature,
and Fiction

Children's Room

KEY

?	Information Desk
	Men's Room
	Women's Room
	Handicap Access
	Check out/ Library Cards
	Telephone
	Returns
	Card Catalog
	Computerized Catalog
	Photocopier
	Elevator
	Stairs

Videos

Art and Music

Periodicals

History and Biography

Newspapers

—DOWNTOWN GAZETTE—
CLASSIFIEDS

Find it, buy it, sell it, or whatever! To place your ad in the *Downtown Gazette* Classifieds, call Ms. Melendez, 555-8000.

HELP WANTED

Office Assistant for downtown business. Good phone manner, word processing skills nec. Flexible hours. Call Ms. Bellis 555-7124.

Newspaper Delivery—Deliver the *Downtown Gazette!* Routes open in North End and Old Town. Ideal for students. Call Mr. Margolies 555-5827.

Services Available

No Job Too Small! Painting, carpentry, general handywork. Reasonable rates. Call for free estimates. Maggie 555-4025.

Reliable dog walker available. Let me help your pet get needed exercise. I am a caring and responsible teenager who loves dogs. References available. Call Josh 555-4382.

PETS FOR ADOPTION

Our dog, Max, needs a new home (our baby has allergies). He is a 6-year-old cocker/poodle mix, healthy, playful, affectionate. Call Jason or Myra 555-8099.

AKC-registered German shepherd puppies. $50. Call after 6 PM. 555-1296.

EVENTS

Want to celebrate the good weather? Need to sing and stomp your feet? Take the family to an outdoor Children's Concert, Sunday April 19, 4 PM (rain or shine!). In the large yard at Community Hall, 434 Main St. Admission $1 for children under 12, $2 for teenagers and adults. Refreshments available. Proceeds to benefit the Fund to Fix Our Playgrounds. For further information, call 555-8937.

TAG SALES

Large variety of children's goods for sale—clothing, toys, books. Saturday April 18, 10 AM–6 PM (raindate Sunday April 19). 85 Elm St.

We did our Spring Cleaning! Come find a treasure! Furniture, antiques, bicycles, small appliances, clothing, dishes. Sunday April 19, 10 AM–5 PM (raindate Sunday April 26). 14 Mountain Ave.

Schedules

SAN FRANCISCO TO SAN JOSE

			TRAIN NO. — AM		TRAIN NO. — PM						
MILES	ZONE	STATION	92	40	44	48	94	98	76	78	80
0.0		Lv San Francisco @ 4th & Townsend Sts.	8:00	10:00	Noon	2:00	4:00	6:00	7:15	8:00	10:00
1.9	SF	Lv 22nd Street	8:05	10:05	12:05	2:05	4:05	6:05	7:20	8:05	10:05
4.1		Lv Paul Avenue	8:09	—	—	—	4:09	6:09	—	—	—
5.2		Lv Bayshore	8:12	10:10	12:10	2:10	4:12	6:12	7:25	8:10	10:10
9.3		Lv So. San Francisco	8:17	10:15	12:15	2:15	4:17	6:17	7:30	8:15	10:15
11.6	1	Lv San Bruno	8:21	10:19	12:19	2:19	4:21	6:21	7:34	8:19	10:19
13.7		Lv Millbrae	8:25	10:23	12:23	2:23	4:25	6:25	7:38	8:23	10:23
15.2		Lv Broadway	8:28	10:26	12:26	2:26	4:28	6:28	7:41	8:26	10:26
16.3		Lv Burlingame	8:31	10:28	12:28	2:28	4:30	6:30	7:44	8:28	10:28
17.9	2	Lv San Mateo	8:34	10:31	12:31	2:31	4:33	6:33	7:47	8:31	10:31
18.9		Lv Hayward Park	8:36	10:34	12:34	2:34	4:36	6:36	7:50	8:34	10:34
20.0		Lv Bay Meadows ●	—	—	—	—	—	—	—	—	—
20.3		Lv Hillsdale	8:39	10:37	12:37	2:37	4:39	6:39	7:53	8:37	10:37
21.9		Lv Belmont	8:42	10:40	12:40	2:40	4:42	6:42	7:56	8:40	10:40
23.2	3	Lv San Carlos	8:45	10:43	12:43	2:43	4:45	6:45	7:59	8:43	10:43
25.4		Lv Redwood City	8:49	10:47	12:47	2:47	4:49	6:49	8:03	8:47	10:47
27.8		Lv Atherton	8:53	10:51	12:51	2:51	4:53	6:53	8:07	8:51	10:51
28.9		Lv Menlo Park	8:56	10:53	12:53	2:53	4:55	6:55	8:10	8:53	10:53
30.1		Lv Palo Alto	8:59	10:56	12:56	2:56	4:58	6:58	8:13	8:56	10:56
31.8	4	Lv Stanford Stadium ●	—	—	—	—	—	—	—	—	—
34.8		Lv California Avenue	9:02	10:59	12:59	2:59	5:01	7:01	8:16	8:59	10:59
36.1		Lv Mountain View	9:08	11:05	1:05	3:05	5:07	7:07	8:22	9:05	11:05
38.8		Lv Sunnyvale	9:12	11:09	1:09	3:09	5:11	7:11	8:26	9:09	11:09
40.8	5	Lv Lawrence	9:16	11:12	1:12	3:12	5:15	7:15	8:30	9:12	11:12
44.3		Lv Santa Clara	9:20	11:17	1:17	3:17	5:19	7:19	8:35	9:17	11:17
46.9		Ar San Jose	9:28	11:25	1:25	3:25	5:28	7:28	8:43	9:25	11:25
	🚌	Ar Santa Cruz	10:30	12:30	2:30	4:30	6:40	8:30		10:30	

🚌   Indicates bus connection to Santa Cruz.

*   New Year's Day, Memorial Day, Independence Day, Labor Day, Thanksgiving Day and Christmas Day. (CalTrain may operate reduced service on holiday eves and day after Thanksgiving). Call the CalTrain Hotline for details.

●   Special train service during racing, football, Giants baseball seasons only.

GLOS

This glossary can help you to pronounce and find out the meanings of words in this book that you may not know.

The words are listed in alphabetical order. Guide words at the top of each page tell you the first and last words on the page.

Each word is divided into syllables. The way to pronounce each word is given next. You can understand the pronunciation respelling by using the key at right. A shorter key appears at the bottom of every other page.

When a word has more than one syllable, a dark accent mark (′) shows which syllable is stressed. In some words, a light accent mark (′) shows which syllable has a less heavy stress.

Glossary entries are based on entries in *The Macmillan/McGraw-Hill School Dictionary 1*.

a at, bad	**d** dear, soda, bad
ā ape, pain, day, break	**f** five, defend, leaf, off, cough, elephant
ä father, car, heart	
âr care, pair, bear, their, where	**g** game, ago, fog, egg
e end, pet, said, heaven, friend	**h** hat, ahead
ē equal, me, feet, team, piece, key	**hw** white, whether, which
i it, big, English, hymn	**j** joke, enjoy, gem, page, edge
ī ice, fine, lie, my	**k** kite, bakery, seek, tack, cat
îr ear, deer, here, pierce	**l** lid, sailor, feel, ball, allow
o odd, hot, watch	**m** man, family, dream
ō old, oat, toe, low	**n** not, final, pan, knife
ô coffee, all, taught, law, fought	**ng** long, singer, pink
ôr order, fork, horse, story, pour	**p** pail, repair, soap, happy
oi oil, toy	**r** ride, parent, wear, more, marry
ou out, now	**s** sit, aside, pets, cent, pass
u up, mud, love, double	**sh** shoe, washer, fish, mission, nation
ū use, mule, cue, feud, few	**t** tag, pretend, fat, button, dressed
ü rule, true, food	**th** thin, panther, both
u̇ put, wood, should	**th** this, mother, smooth
ûr burn, hurry, term, bird, word, courage	**v** very, favor, wave
	w wet, weather, reward
ə about, taken, pencil, lemon, circus	**y** yes, onion
b bat, above, job	**z** zoo, lazy, jazz, rose, dogs, houses
ch chin, such, match	**zh** vision, treasure, seizure

absorb To soak up or take in. A towel *absorbed* the spilled water.
ab•sorb (ab sôrb′ *or* ab zôrb′) *verb*, **absorbed, absorbing.**

Amazon The longest river in South America and, by volume, the largest in the world, flowing from the Andes across Brazil into the Atlantic. Its length is about 4,000 mi. (6,436 km).
Am•a•zon (am′ə zon′) *noun.*

ancestor A person from whom one is descended. Your grandparents and great-grandparents are among your *ancestors.*
an•ces•tor (an′ses tər) *noun,* plural **ancestors.**

Word History

The word **ancestor** comes from the French word *ancêtre* with the same meaning. This French word comes from the Latin words *ante-,* meaning "before" and *cēdere,* meaning "to go."

---

appear 1. To come into sight; be seen. The snowy mountain peaks *appeared* in the distance. **2.** To give the impression of being; look. They *appeared* interested in the game, but they were really bored.
ap•pear (ə pîr′) *verb,* **appeared, appearing.**

appreciate 1. To understand the value of. Everyone *appreciates* loyal friends. **2.** To be grateful for something. I *appreciate* your running these errands for me.
ap•pre•ci•ate (ə prē′shē āt′) *verb,* **appreciated, appreciating.**

aquarium 1. A tank, bowl, or similar container in which fish, other water animals, and water plants are kept. An aquarium is usually made of glass or some other material that one can see through. **2.** A building used to display collections of fish, other water animals, and water plants.
a•quar•i•um (ə kwar′ē əm) *noun,* plural **aquariums.**

aquarium

argue 1. To have a difference of opinion; disagree. My parents always *argue* about politics. **2.** To give reasons for or against something. I *argued* against going to the beach because it looked like it might rain.
ar•gue (är′gū) *verb,* **argued, arguing.**

arrangements Plans or preparations. Our class made *arrangements* to visit the zoo.
ar•range•ments (ə rānj′mənts) *plural noun.*

assorted Of many kinds. The bakery has a display of *assorted* cookies.
as•sort•ed (ə sôr′tid) *adjective.*

B

bamboo A tall plant that is related to grass. The bamboo has woody stems that are often hollow and are used to make fishing poles, canes, and furniture. *Noun.*
—Made of *bamboo*. *Adjective.*
  bam•boo (bam bü′) *noun, plural* **bamboos;** *adjective.*

Word History
The word **bamboo** comes from the Malay word *bambu* for the same plant.

bamboo

Bapa Raja (bä′pə rä′jə).

beneath 1. Lower than; below; under. We stood *beneath* the stars. **2.** Unworthy of. Telling a lie is *beneath* you.
  be•neath (bi nēth′) *preposition.*

bore To make a hole in. The carpenter *bored* the wood with a drill. ▲ Another word that sounds like this is **boar.**
  bore (bôr) *verb,* **bored, boring.**

bough A large branch of a tree. We fastened the swing to a *bough* of the tree. ▲ Two other words that sound like this are **bow** (verb) and **bow** (noun).
  bough (bou) *noun, plural* **boughs.**

bound¹ 1. To leap; spring; jump. The rabbit *bounded* away into the woods. **2.** To spring back after hitting something. The ball *bounded* off the wall and hit my bicycle.
  bound (bound) *verb,* **bounded, bounding.**

bound² 1. Fastened; tied. The bank robbers left the guard *bound* and gagged. **2.** Have a duty or responsibility. I am *bound* by my promise to keep the secret.
  bound (bound) *adjective.*

Buddhist Relating to Buddhism, a religion that is based on the teachings of Buddha, an Indian religious leader who lived from about 563 B.C. to about 483 B.C.
  Bud•dhist (bủd′ist *or* bü′dist) *adjective.*

buffalo A large North American animal that has a big hump on its back; bison. Many years ago *buffalo* roamed free on the plains.
  buf•fa•lo (buf′ə lō) *noun, plural* **buffaloes** or **buffalos** or **buffalo.**

---

at; āpe; fär; câre; end; mē; it; īce; pîerce; hot; ōld; sông; fôrk; oil; out; up; ūse; rüle; pủll; tûrn; chin; sing; shop; thin; this; hw in white; zh in treasure. The symbol ə stands for the unstressed vowel sound in about, taken, pencil, lemon, and circus.

C

cactus A plant that has a thick stem covered with spines instead of leaves. Cacti are found in desert areas of North and South America. Most cacti produce bright flowers and edible fruit.
    cac•tus (kak′təs) *noun, plural* **cacti** (kak′tī), **cactuses,** or **cactus.**

cactus

Camila (kä mē′lä).

Caracas The capital and largest city of Venezuela, in the northern part of the country.
    Ca•rac•as (kə rä′kəs).

Carlitos (kär lē′tōs).

catalogue A list. Stores publish catalogues with pictures and prices of the things they have for sale.
    cat•a•logue (kat′ə lôg′) *noun, plural* **catalogues.**

cellar A room or group of rooms built underground. Most *cellars* are under buildings and are used for storage.
    cel•lar (sel′ər) *noun, plural* **cellars.**

Cheo (chā′ō).

Chew and swallow (chü′ ənd swol′ō).

command 1. To give an order to; direct. The trainer commanded the dog to sit still. **2.** To have power over; rule. The general *commands* the army.
    com•mand (kə mand′) *verb,* **commanded, commanding.**

committee A group of persons who are chosen to do certain work. The decorations committee decorated the gym for the school dance.
    com•mit•tee (kə mit′ē) *noun, plural* **committees.**

community 1. A group of different plants and animals that live together in the same area and depend on one another for their survival. **2.** A group of people who live together in the same place. Our *community* voted to build a new library.
    com•mu•ni•ty (kə mū′ni tē) *noun, plural* **communities.**

company 1. Companionship. When the rest of the family is away, I am grateful for my dog's *company.* **2.** A guest or guests. **3.** A business firm or organization. My father's *company* is located in New York.
    com•pa•ny (kum′pə nē) *noun, plural* **companies.**

complicated Hard to understand or do. The directions for putting together the bicycle were too *complicated* for me to follow.
    com•pli•cat•ed (kom′pli kā′tid) *adjective.*

cooperate To work together. The three classes *cooperated* in planning a picnic at the end of the school year.
　　co•op•er•ate (kō op′ə rāt′) *verb,* **cooperated, cooperating.**

> **Word History**
> The word **cooperate** comes from co-, a Latin word beginning that means "together," and the Latin word *operari,* meaning "to work."

coral A hard substance that is like stone and is found in tropical seas. Coral is made up of the skeletons of tiny sea animals. *Noun.*
—Made of *coral.* A *coral* reef surrounds the island. *Adjective.*
　　cor•al (kôr′əl) *noun; adjective.*

coral

creature A living person or animal. Deer, bears, and wolves are *creatures* of the forest.
　　crea•ture (krē′chər) *noun, plural* **creatures.**

crouch To stoop or bend low with the knees bent. The cat *crouched* in the bushes.
　　crouch (krouch) *verb,* **crouched, crouching.**

curious Eager to learn about things that are new, strange, or interesting. I was really *curious* about those dinosaur bones.
　　cu•ri•ous (kyùr′ē əs) *adjective.*

customer A person who buys something at a store or uses the services of a business. Most of the bakery's regular *customers* shop there at least once a week.
　　cus•tom•er (kus′tə mər) *noun, plural* **customers.**

D

damage Harm or injury that makes something less valuable or useful. The flood caused great *damage* to the farms in the area.
　　dam•age (dam′ij) *noun, plural* **damages.**

dare **1.** To be bold enough to try; have the courage for. No one *dared* to go into the dark cave. **2.** To ask someone to do something as a test of courage or ability; challenge.
　　dare (dâr) *verb,* **dared, daring.**

dedicate To set apart or devote to a special purpose or use. Many scientists have *dedicated* themselves to finding a cure for cancer.
　　ded•i•cate (ded′i kāt′) *verb,* **dedicated, dedicating.**

> at; āpe; fär; câre; end; mē; it; īce; pîerce; hot; ōld; sông; fôrk; oil; out; up; ūse; rüle; pùll; tûrn; chin; sing; shop; thin; this; hw in white; zh in treasure. The symbol ə stands for the unstressed vowel sound in about, taken, pencil, lemon, and circus.

G5

demand To ask for urgently or forcefully. The customers *demanded* their money back for the broken radio.
    de•mand (di mand') *verb*, **demanded, demanding.**

depend **1.** To rely or trust. You can always *depend* on my friend to be on time. **2.** To get help or support. Children *depend* on their parents. **3.** To be determined by how something else turns out. Whether we go on the hike *depends* on the weather.
    de•pend (di pend') *verb*, **depended, depending.**

desert¹ A hot, dry, sandy area of land with few or no plants growing on it.
    des•ert (dez'ərt) *noun*, *plural* **deserts.**

desert

desert² To go away and leave a person or thing that should not be left; abandon. The soldiers *deserted* their company.
    de•sert (di zûrt') *verb*, **deserted, deserting.**

destroy To ruin completely; wreck. The earthquake *destroyed* the city.
    de•stroy (di stroi') *verb*, **destroyed, destroying.**

determined Firm in sticking to a purpose. The *determined* students kept phoning the senator's office until somebody answered.
    de•ter•mined (di tûr'mind) *adjective*.

develop **1.** To come gradually into being. A rash *developed* on the baby's skin. **2.** To grow or cause to grow; expand. You can *develop* your muscles by exercising.
    de•vel•op (di vel'əp) *verb*, **developed, developing.**

discuss To talk over; speak about. We *discussed* our favorite book.
    dis•cuss (di skus') *verb*, **discussed, discussing.**

drench To make something completely wet; soaked. The big wave *drenched* the children on the raft.
    drench (drench) *verb*, **drenched, drenching.**

echo The repeating of a sound. Echoes are caused when sound waves bounce off a surface. We shouted "hello" toward the hill and soon heard the *echo* of our voices.
    ech•o (ek'ō) *noun*, *plural* **echoes.**

election The act of choosing by voting. There is an *election* for the president every four years in the United States.
    e•lec•tion (i lek'shən) *noun*, *plural* **elections.**

environment 1. The air, the water, the soil, and all the other things that surround a person, animal, or plant. The *environment* can affect the growth and health of living things. **2.** Surroundings; atmosphere. The library provided a quiet *environment* for me to work.
en•vi•ron•ment (en vī′ rən mənt *or* en vī′ərn mənt) *noun, plural* **environments.**

especially More than usual. Be *especially* careful to not slip on the icy sidewalk.
es•pe•cial•ly (e spesh′ə lē) *adverb.*

exclaim To speak or shout suddenly, or with force; to express surprise or other strong feeling. "My bicycle's missing!" I *exclaimed.*
ex•claim (ek sklām′) *verb,* **exclaimed, exclaiming.**

Exxon Valdez (ek′son val dēz′ *or* väl dez′).

F

flutter To move or fly with quick, light, flapping movements. Butterflies *fluttered* among the flowers.
flut•ter (flut′ər) *verb,* **fluttered, fluttering.**

flutter

frequent Happening often; taking place again and again. There are *frequent* thunderstorms in this area.
fre•quent (frē′kwənt) *adjective.*

G

gaze To look at something a long time. We *gazed* at the sunset.
gaze (gāz) *verb,* **gazed, gazing.**

generation One step in the line of descent from a common relative. A grandparent, parent, and child make up three *generations.*
gen•er•a•tion (jen′ə rā′shən) *noun, plural* **generations.**

gradual Happening little by little; moving or changing slowly. We watched the *gradual* growth of the plants in our vegetable garden.
grad•u•al (graj′ü əl) *adjective.*

H

hesitate To wait or stop a moment, especially because of feeling unsure. The speaker *hesitated* and looked down at his notes.
hes•i•tate (hez′i tāt′) *verb,* **hesitated, hesitating.**

at; āpe; fär; câre; end; mē; it; īce; pîerce; hot; ōld; sông; fôrk; oil; out; up; ūse; rüle; púll; tûrn; chin; sing; shop; thin; this; hw in white; zh in treasure. The symbol ə stands for the unstressed vowel sound in about, taken, pencil, lemon, and circus.

hoarse Having a deep, rough, or harsh sound. The teacher's voice was *hoarse* from a bad cold.
▲ Another word that sounds like this is **horse.**
   hoarse (hôrs) *adjective,* **hoarser, hoarsest.**

hollow 1. Having a hole or an empty space inside; not solid. A water pipe is *hollow.* **2.** Curved in like a cup or bowl; sunken.
   hol•low (hol′ō) *adjective,* **hollower, hollowest.**

honor To show or feel great respect for a person or thing. The city *honored* the president with a parade.
   hon•or (on′ər) *verb,* **honored, honoring.**

I

imagine 1. To picture a person or thing in the mind. Try to *imagine* a dragon breathing fire. **2.** To suppose; guess. I don't *imagine* we will go on a picnic if it rains.
   i•mag•ine (i maj′in) *verb,* **imagined, imagining.**

immediately Right away; now. If we leave *immediately,* we can get to the movie in time.
   im•me•di•ate•ly (i mē′dē it lē) *adverb.*

innocent 1. Not doing harm; harmless. The children hid from their parents as an *innocent* joke. **2.** Free from guilt or wrong. An *innocent* person was accused of the crime, but a jury found the person not guilty.
   in•no•cent (in′ə sənt) *adjective.*

insect Any of a large group of small animals without a backbone. The body of an insect is divided into three parts. Insects have three pairs of legs and usually two pairs of wings. Flies, ants, grasshoppers, and beetles are *insects.*
   in•sect (in′sekt) *noun, plural* **insects.**

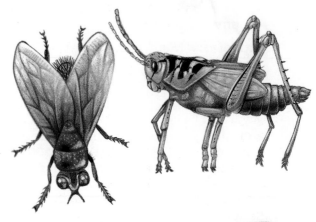

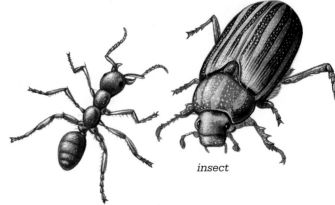

insect

insert To put or place in. I *inserted* a coin in the vending machine. *Verb.*
—Something put or placed in. The Sunday edition of the newspaper has an eight-page color *insert* on vacations. *Noun.*
   in•sert (in sûrt′) *verb,* **inserted, inserting;** *noun, plural* **inserts.**

insist To demand or say in a strong, firm manner. The doctor *insisted* that the sick patient stayed in bed.
   in•sist (in sist′) *verb,* **insisted, insisting.**

intelligent Having or showing the ability to think, learn, and understand. *Intelligent* people often learn from their mistakes and do not repeat them.
   in•tel•li•gent (in tel′i jənt) *adjective.*

J

jaguar A large animal that belongs to the cat family. The short fur of the jaguar is golden and is marked with black rings with spots in their centers. Jaguars are found in Mexico, Central America, and South America. The *jaguar* ran across the grassy plain.
   jag•uar (jag′wär) *noun, plural* **jaguars.**

Word History

   The word **jaguar** comes from the Spanish word *yaguar* and the Portugese word *jaguar,* which in turn came from the languages of the Guarani and Tupi Native Americans of the Amazon region.

---

jungle 1. Land in tropical areas that is covered with a thick mass of trees, vines, and bushes. Much of the Amazon River in Brazil runs through the dense *jungle.* **2.** Any wild, confused, or tangled growth or area. The city was a *jungle* of streets and skyscrapers.
   jun•gle (jung′gəl) *noun, plural* **jungles.**

K

kapok A tropical tree that produces a light, fluffy fiber used as a stuffing for life preservers, pillows, and mattresses.
   ka•pok (kā′pok) *noun.*

kapok

Kitamura (ke tä mü′ rä).

L

Leonardo da Vinci 1452-1519, Italian artist and scientist. One of his most famous paintings is the *Mona Lisa.*
   Le•o•nar•do da Vin•ci (lē′ə när′dō də vin′chē) *noun.*

---

at; āpe; fär; câre; end; mē; it; īce; pîerce; hot; ōld; sông; fôrk; oil; out; up; ūse; rüle; pull; tûrn; chin; sing; shop; thin; **th**is; **hw** in **wh**ite; **zh** in trea**s**ure. The symbol ə stands for the unstressed vowel sound in **a**bout, tak**e**n, penc**i**l, lem**o**n, and circ**u**s.

---

librarian A person who is in charge of or works in a library. The *librarian* helped me find books for my report.

li•brar•i•an (lī brâr′ē ən) *noun*, *plural* **librarians.**

M

memory 1. All that a person can remember. The student flawlessly recited the poem from *memory.* **2.** The ability to remember things. Maria has a good *memory.* **3.** A person or thing that is remembered. I have some good *memories* of my great-grandmother.

mem•o•ry (mem′ə rē) *noun*, *plural* **memories.**

miracle 1. An amazing or wonderful thing. It was a *miracle* that our team won the championship. **2.** Something amazing or wonderful that cannot be explained by the laws of nature. It was a *miracle* she survived the shipwreck, because she cannot swim.

mir•a•cle (mir′ə kəl) *noun*, *plural* **miracles.**

Miyo (mē′yō).

moist Slightly wet; damp. I wiped the shelves with a *moist* cloth.

moist (moist) *adjective*, **moister, moistest.**

molecule The smallest particle into which a substance can be divided without being changed chemically. For example, a *molecule* of water has two atoms of hydrogen and one atom of oxygen.

mol•e•cule (mol′ə kūl′) *noun*, *plural* **molecules.**

N

natural 1. Not resulting from teaching or training. The new sergeant was a *natural* leader. **2.** Found in nature; not made by people; not artificial. *Natural* rock formations overlook the river.

nat•u•ral (nach′ər əl) *adjective.*

necessity Something that cannot be done without; requirement. Food, clothing, and shelter are the *necessities* of life.

ne•ces•si•ty (ni ses′i tē) *noun*, *plural* **necessities.**

necklace A string of beads or other jewelry that is worn around the neck for decoration.

neck•lace (nek′lis) *noun*, *plural* **necklaces.**

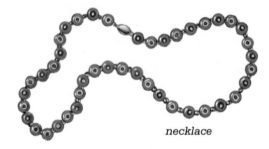

necklace

O

occasional Happening or appearing now and then; not frequent. The weather report said there will be *occasional* showers today.

oc•ca•sion•al (ə kā′zhə nəl) *adjective.*

occur 1. To take place; happen. The fire *occurred* in the middle of the night. **2.** To come into one's thoughts. It did not *occur* to me to take my umbrella.
oc•cur (ə kûr′) *verb*, **occurred, occurring.**

offer 1. The act of presenting something to be accepted or turned down. We accept your *offer* of help. **2.** Something presented to be accepted or turned down. The salesman turned down our *offer* of $500 for the old car.
of•fer (ô′fər) *noun, plural* **offers.**

P

pardon 1. The act of refusing to blame or punish; forgiveness. I beg your *pardon* if I hurt you. **2.** A freeing from punishment. The prisoner received a *pardon* from the governor.
par•don (pär′dən) *noun, plural* **pardons.**

particular 1. Taken by itself; apart from others. This *particular* suitcase is too small for me. **2.** Having to do with some one person or thing. This artist's *particular* talent is drawing plants. **3.** Unusual in some way; special. That book should be of *particular* interest to you.
par•tic•u•lar (pər tik′yə lər) *adjective.*

perform 1. To carry out; do. The doctor *performed* the operation. **2.** To sing, act, or do something in public that requires skill. Our band *performed* at the game.
per•form (pər fôrm′) *verb*, **performed, performing.**

permanent A wavy or curly hairdo that lasts several months, set in the hair with a chemical solution or with heat. *Noun.*
—Lasting or meant to last; enduring. After graduating from college, I started looking for a *permanent* job. *Adjective.*
per•ma•nent (pûr′mə nənt) *noun; adjective.*

photograph A picture that is made by using a camera.
pho•to•graph (fō′tə graf′) *noun, plural* **photographs.**

photograph

prediction The act of telling something before it happens. The weather *prediction* I heard on the radio said it would rain this weekend.
pre•dic•tion (pri dik′shən) *noun, plural* **predictions.**

at; āpe; fär; câre; end; mē; it; īce; pîerce; hot; ōld; sông; fôrk; oil; out; up; ūse; rüle; pùll; tûrn; chin; sing; shop; thin; this; hw in white; zh in treasure. The symbol ə stands for the unstressed vowel sound in about, taken, pencil, lemon, and circus.

prepare To make or get ready. We *prepared* for the race by doing some exercises.
 pre•pare (pri pâr′) *verb*, **prepared, preparing.**

pretend 1. To give a false show. The children *pretended* to be asleep. **2.** To make believe. We *pretended* we were sailors on a large ship.
 pre•tend (pri tend′) *verb*, **pretended, pretending.**

prevent 1. To keep something from happening. Putting out campfires helps *prevent* forest fires. **2.** To keep someone from doing something; hinder. The noise outside our window *prevented* us from sleeping.
 pre•vent (pri vent′) *verb*, **prevented, preventing.**

prey 1. The habit of hunting animals for food. A tiger is a beast of *prey.* **2.** An animal that is hunted by another animal for food. Rabbits, birds, and snakes are the *prey* of foxes. ▲ Another word that sounds like this is **pray.**
 prey (prā) *noun.*

prickly Having small, sharp thorns or points. We planted *prickly* rose bushes along the fence.
 prick•ly (prik′lē) *adjective*, **pricklier, prickliest.**

produce 1. To make or create something. That factory *produces* automobiles. **2.** To bring forth; show. The lawyer *produced* new evidence at the trial.
 pro•duce (prə dūs′ *or* prə dūs′) *verb*, **produced, producing.**

pronounce 1. To make the sound of a letter or word. People from different parts of the country *pronounce* certain words differently. **2.** To say or declare. The judge *pronounced* the prisoner not guilty.
 pro•nounce (prə nouns′) *verb*, **pronounced, pronouncing.**

quantity A number or amount. That restaurant buys large *quantities* of food.
 quan•ti•ty (kwon′ti tē) *noun*, *plural* **quantities.**

Word History

 The word **quantity** comes from the French word *quantité*, which in turn came from the Latin word *quantus*, meaning "how much" or "how large."

---

rescue To save or free. The lifeguard *rescued* the drowning child.
 res•cue (res′kū) *verb*, **rescued, rescuing.**

ruins The remains of something destroyed or decayed. They found the *ruins* of an old stone wall.
 ru•ins (rü′inz) *plural noun*

Chichén Itzá ruins

Rumphius (rum′fē əs).

S

San José (san hō zā′).

satisfaction The condition of being given, or the act of giving enough to meet one's needs or desires. Don't you get a lot of *satisfaction* from doing your homework well?
sat•is•fac•tion (sat′is fak′shən) *noun.*

scatter To spread or throw about in many different places. The wind *scattered* the leaves.
scat•ter (skat′ər) *verb,* **scattered, scattering.**

scowl To frown in an angry way. The father *scowled* at his child's rude behavior.
scowl (skoul) *verb,* **scowled, scowling.**

scrub To rub in order to wash or clean. You'll have to *scrub* your hands to get them clean.
scrub (skrub) *verb,* **scrubbed, scrubbing.**

scurry To go or move in a hurry. The children *scurried* after their parents.
scur•ry (skûr′ē) *verb,* **scurried, scurrying.**

seashore The land near or on the sea. We walked along the *seashore* and collected many beautiful shells.
sea•shore (sē′shôr′) *noun, plural* **seashores.**

Senhor Sir; mister. The Portuguese form of polite address for a man. The Portuguese language is spoken in Portugal, Brazil, and other countries.
se•nhor (si nyōr′ *or* si nyôr′) *noun.*

shaggy Long, bushy, and rough. That dog's hair is very *shaggy.*
shag•gy (shag′ē) *adjective,* **shaggier, shaggiest.**

shaggy

shelter To cover or protect. The tent *sheltered* us.
shel•ter (shel′tər) *verb,* **sheltered, sheltering.**

silent 1. Completely quiet; still. She crept through the *silent* house. 2. Not speaking, or saying little. The children remained *silent* during the play.
si•lent (sī′lənt) *adjective.*

species A group of animals or plants that have many characteristics in common. Poodles and beagles belong to the same *species.*
spe•cies (spē′shēz) *noun, plural* **species.**

at; āpe; fär; câre; end; mē; it; īce; pîerce; hot; ōld; sông; fôrk; oil; out; up; ūse; rüle; pùll; tûrn; chin; sing; shop; thin; **th**is; **hw** in **wh**ite; **zh** in trea**s**ure. The symbol ə stands for the unstressed vowel sound in about, taken, pencil, lemon, and circus.

squawk 1. To make a shrill, harsh cry like that of a frightened chicken. The parrot *squawked* when I waved a cracker in front of it. **2.** To complain loudly or harshly. Don't *squawk* about your chores.
 squawk (skwôk) *verb,* **squawked, squawking.**

startle To excite or cause to move suddenly, as with surprise or fright. A spider dropped from the ceiling and *startled* me.
 star•tle (stär'təl) *verb,* **startled, startling.**

suggest 1. To offer as something to think about. Who *suggested* that we play baseball? **2.** To come or bring into the mind. The color red *suggests* warmth. **3.** To hint. Your smile *suggests* that you are happy.
 sug•gest (səg jest' *or* sə jest') *verb,* **suggested, suggesting.**

Sun Ho (sun hō).

supply To provide with something needed or wanted. Rain *supplies* water. *Verb.*
—A quantity of something that is needed or ready for use. We have bought the *supplies* for our camping trip. *Noun.*
 sup•ply (sə plī') *verb,* **supplied, supplying;** *noun, plural* **supplies.**

suspend 1. To attach so as to hang down. The swing was *suspended* from a branch. **2.** To support while allowing movement. Bits of lemon were *suspended* in the lemonade.
 sus•pend (sə spend') *verb,* **suspended, suspending.**

Word History

The word **suspend** comes from the Latin word *suspendere,* which is made up of *sus-,* a Latin word beginning that means "up," and the Latin word *pendere,* meaning "to cause to hang."

T

Tami (tä' mē).

temple¹ A building that is used for the worship of a god or gods. Long ago, the Romans built this *temple* as a place to pray to their gods.
 tem•ple (tem'pəl) *noun, plural* **temples.**

temple

temple² The flattened part on either side of the forehead. The *temple* is above the cheek and in front of the ear.
 tem•ple (tem'pəl) *noun, plural* **temples.**

twilight The time just after sunset or just before sunrise when there is a soft, hazy light.
 twi•light (twī'līt) *noun.*

twist 1. To wind or turn around something. The dog's chain was *twisted* around the tree. **2.** To change the meaning of; distort. He *twisted* our words.
> **twist** (twist) *verb,* **twisted, twisting.**

V

valuable 1. Having great use or importance. My summer job was a *valuable* experience for me. **2.** Worth much money. The museum has a very *valuable* collection of paintings.
> **val•u•a•ble** (val′ū ə bəl *or* val′yə bəl) *adjective.*

Venezuela A country in northern South America.
> **Ven•e•zue•la** (ven′ə zwā′lə *or* ven′ə zwē′lə) *noun.*

Venezuela

vent A hole or other opening through which a gas or liquid passes in order to get out of somewhere. A *vent* above the stove lets air out of the kitchen.
> **vent** (vent) *noun, plural* **vents.**

volunteer A person who offers to help, or does something by choice, and often without pay. The teacher asked for *volunteers* for the book fair committee. *Noun*
—**1.** To offer to help or do something of one's own free will. My friend *volunteered* to coach the baseball team. **2.** To give or offer readily. I *volunteered* an answer to the question. *Verb.*
> **vol•un•teer** (vol′ən tîr′) *noun, plural* **volunteers;** *verb* **volunteered, volunteering.**

W

warning Notice or advice given beforehand of a danger or possible bad result. The *warning* on the label said the bottle contained poison.
> **warn•ing** (wôr′ning) *noun, plural* **warnings.**

whimper To cry with weak broken sounds. The puppy *whimpered* for it's mother
> **whim•per** (hwim′pər *or* wim′pər) *verb,* **whimpered, whimpering.**

---

at; āpe; fär; câre; end; mē; it; īce; pîerce; hot; ōld; sông; fôrk; oil; out; up; ūse; rüle; pull; tûrn; **ch**in; sin**g**; **sh**op; **th**in; **th**is; **hw** in **wh**ite; **zh** in treasure. The symbol ə stands for the unstressed vowel sound in **a**bout, tak**e**n, penc**i**l, lem**o**n, and circ**u**s.

---

whirl To turn or cause to turn quickly in a circle. The blades of a fan *whirl* and create a cooling breeze.
> **whirl** (hwûrl *or* wûrl) *verb,* **whirled, whirling.**

wither To dry up and become wrinkled. Put the cut flowers in water before they *wither.*
> **with•er** (wi<u>th</u>′ər) *verb,* **withered, withering.**

Yanomamo A tribe of people who live in the rain forest of Brazil.
> **Ya•no•ma•mo** (yä′nō mä′mō) *noun.*

Young Mee (yung mē).

ACKNOWLEDGMENTS

The publisher gratefully acknowledges permission to reprint the following copyrighted material:

"All the Ones They Call Lowly" by David Campbell from A CARIBBEAN DOZEN. Edited by John Agard & Grace Nichols. Illustrations © 1994 Cathie Felstead. Permission granted by Walker Books Limited, London. Published in the U.S. by Candlewick Press, Cambridge, MA.

"And my heart soars" by Chief Dan George. Copyright © 1974 by Chief Dan George and Helmut Hirnschall. Reprinted by permission of Hancock House Publishing Ltd. 19313 Zeroz Ave., Surrey, BC V3S 5J9, Canada.

Illustration from BEAT THE STORY DRUM, PUM-PUM retold and illustrated by Ashley Bryan. Copyright © 1980 Ashley Bryan. Reprinted with permission of Atheneum Books for Young Readers, an imprint of Simon & Schuster Children's Publishing Division.

"Cactus Hotel" from CACTUS HOTEL text by Brenda Z. Guiberson, illustrated by Megan Lloyd. Text copyright © 1991 by Brenda Guiberson. Illustrations copyright © 1991 by Megan Lloyd. Reprinted by permission of Henry Holt and Co.

"Cloudy With a Chance of Meatballs" is from CLOUDY WITH A CHANCE OF MEATBALLS by Judi Barrett. Copyright © 1978 by Judi Barrett, illustrations copyright © 1978 by Ron Barrett. Reprinted with permission from Atheneum Books for Young Readers, an imprint of Simon & Schuster Children's Publishing Division.

Illustration from THE DANCING GRANNY retold and illustrated by Ashley Bryan. Copyright © 1977 by Ashley Bryan. Reprinted with permission of Atheneum Books for Young Readers, an imprint of Simon & Schuster Children's Publishing Division.

"Dream Wolf" is from DREAM WOLF by Paul Goble. Copyright © 1990 by Paul Goble. Reprinted with the permission of Simon & Schuster Books For Young Readers.

"A Fruit & Vegetable Man" from A FRUIT & VEGETABLE MAN by Roni Schotter. Text Copyright © 1993 by Roni Schotter; Illustrations copyright © 1993 by Jeanette Winter. By permission of Little, Brown and Company.

Cover permission for THE GIRL WHO LOVED WILD HORSES by Paul Goble. Copyright 1978 by Paul Goble. Reprinted with the permission of Simon & Schuster Books For Young Readers.

"Gone" from ONE AT A TIME by David McCord. Copyright © 1970 by David McCord. By permission of Little, Brown and Company.

"The Great Kapok Tree" from THE GREAT KAPOK TREE: A TALE OF THE AMAZON RAIN FOREST, copyright © 1990 by Lynne Cherry, reprinted by permission of Harcourt Brace & Company.

"An Incredible Journey" Water cycle board game adapted from "An Incredible Journey" in the Project Wet Curriculum and Activity Guide a publication of Project WET. Illustration by Peter Grosshauer.

"In Memory" by Ericka Northrop from JACK AND JILL, copyright © 1989 by Children's Better Health Institute, Benjamin Franklin Literary & Medical Society, Inc., Indianapolis, Indiana. Used by permission.

"In Time of Silver Rain" from SELECTED POEMS by Langston Hughes. Copyright © 1938 and renewed 1966 by Langston Hughes. Reprinted by permission of Alfred A. Knopf Inc.

Cover permission for ISLAND BOY by Barbara Cooney. Copyright © 1988 by Barbara Cooney Porter. Used by permission by Viking Penguin, a division of Penguin Books, USA Inc.

Illustration from LION AND THE OSTRICH CHICKS retold and illustrated by Ashley Bryan. Copyright © 1986 by Ashley Bryan. Reprinted with permission of Atheneum Books for Young Readers, an imprint of Simon & Schuster Children's Publishing Division.

"Miss Rumphius" from MISS RUMPHIUS by Barbara Cooney. Copyright © 1982 by Barbara Cooney Porter. Used by permission of Viking Penguin, a division of Penguin Books USA, Inc.

"Operation Rescue: Saving Sea Life from Oil Spills" by Christina Wilsdon. Copyright 1990 Children's Television Workshop (New York, New York). All rights reserved.

Cover permission for OX-CART MAN by Donald Hall, illustrated by Barbara Cooney. Copyright © 1979 by Barbara Cooney Porter for illustrations. Used by permission of Viking Penguin, a division of Penguin Books USA Inc.

"Preserven el Parque Elysian" by Mike Kellin. Copyright © 1965 (renewed) by APPLESEED MUSIC INC. All Rights Reserved. Used by Permission.

"Que llueva!"/"It's Raining" from ARROZ CON LECHE by Lulu Delacre. Copyright © 1989 by Lulu Delacre. English lyrics by Elena Paz. Reprinted by permission of Scholastic, Inc.

"Rain Forests Around the World" from WHY SAVE THE RAIN FOREST. Text © 1993 by Donald Silver. Illustrations © 1993 by Patricia Wynne. Silver Burdett Press, Simon & Schuster Elementary Group. Used by permission.

"The Rains in Little Dribbles" from SOMETHING BIG HAS BEEN HERE by Jack Prelutsky. Copyright © 1990 by Jack Prelutsky. Published by Greenwillow Books. Reprinted by permission.

"The Rooster Who Understood Japanese" is from THE ROOSTER WHO UNDERSTOOD JAPANESE by Yoshiko Uchida. Text copyright © 1976 by Yoshiko Uchida. Reprinted courtesy of the Bancroft Library University of California, Berkeley.

"Spring Rain" is from RHYMES ABOUT US by Marchette Chute. Published 1974 by E.P. Dutton. Copyright © 1974 by Marchette Chute. Reprinted by permission of Elizabeth Roach.

"Storm in the Night" is from STORM IN THE NIGHT by Mary Stolz. Text copyright © 1988 by Mary Stolz. Illustrations copyright © 1988 by Pat Cummings. Reprinted by permission of HarperCollins Publishers.

"The Streets Are Free" is from THE STREETS ARE FREE/LA CALLE ES LIBRE by Kurusa, translation Karen Englander. Copyright © 1981 by Ediciones Ekare-Banco del Libro, Caracas, Venezuela. Used by permission of the publisher.

"The Toad" from SPEAKING OF COWS AND OTHER POEMS by Kaye Starbird. Copyright © 1960, © renewed 1988 by Kaye Starbird, Reprinted by permission of Marian Reiner for the author.

"Tornado Alert" Entire text of TORNADO ALERT by Franklyn M. Branley. Text copyright © 1988 by Franklyn M. Branley. Reprinted by permission of HarperCollins Publishers.

"Turtle Knows Your Name" is from TURTLE KNOWS YOUR NAME by Ashley Bryan. Copyright © 1989 by Ashley Bryan. Reprinted by permission of Atheneum Books for Young Readers, an imprint of Simon & Schuster Children's Publishing Division.

"Valentine for Earth" from THE LITTLE NATURALIST by Frances Frost. Copyright © 1959 by Frances Frost. Published by McGraw-Hill. Reprinted by permission.

"Volcanoes" by Judith E. Rand from NATIONAL GEOGRAPHIC WORLD, February 1995. Copyright © 1995 by National Geographic Society.

"Weather Is Full of the Nicest Sounds" from I LIKE WEATHER by Aileen Fisher. Text copyright © 1963 by Aileen Fisher. Reprinted by permission of HarperCollins Publisher.

"Weather Report" by Jane Yolen reprinted by permission of Curtis Brown Ltd. Copyright © 1992 by Jane Yolen. First appeared in WEATHER REPORT. Published by Boyds Mills Press.

"The Wolves of Winter" by Rachel Bucholz, photographs by Jim Brandenburg, from BOY'S LIFE, February 1995. Copyright © 1995 by Boy Scouts of America. Reprinted by permission.

READING RESOURCES

Diagrams: From WEATHER FORECASTING by Gail Gibbons, copyright © 1987 by Gail Gibbons. Reprinted by permission of Four Winds Press, an imprint of Simon & Schuster Books For Young Readers.

Maps: "Indian Groups of North America" from UNITED STATES AND ITS NEIGHBORS, copyright © 1991 by Macmillan/McGraw-Hill School Publishing Company. Reprinted by permission of Macmillan/McGraw-Hill School Publishing Company.

Schedules: Excerpt from CalTrain Peninsula Rail Service timetable. Reprinted by permission of the California Department of Transportation.

COVER DESIGN: Carbone Smolan Associates
COVER ILLUSTRATION: Marc Mongeau

DESIGN CREDITS
Carbone Smolan Associates, front matter, 10-11
Bill Smith Studio, 72-73
Function Thru Form, Inc., 106-110
Notovitz Design Inc., 104-105, 111

ILLUSTRATION CREDITS
Marc Mongeau, 10-11; Susan Huls, 12-13, 29 (borders); Claudia Karabaic Sargent, 32, 34-38, 40-46 (borders); Kathy Jeffers, 48-49 (valentine globe); Grace De Vito, 72-73 (title panel); Leo Kubinyi, 72-73 (map); Steven Bennett, 74 (calligraphy); Jose Ortega, 102-103. **Reading Resources:** Brad Hamann, 104; Maria Lauricella, 106; Steve Sullivan, 107; Bob Mansfield, 108-109. **Glossary:** Lori Anzalone, G3, G4, G7, G8, G10, G13; Greg King, G15.

PHOTOGRAPHY CREDITS
All photographs are by the Macmillan/McGraw-Hill School Division (MMSD) except as noted below.

29: b. Jeannette Winter. 30: m.l. Courtesy of Nathaniel Gallardo. 30-31: m., b.r. Ken Kerbs for MMSD. 46: t. Douglas Merriam. 71: Courtesy Lynne Cherry . 74-75: Ken Straiton/Image Finders. 75: Yorham Kahana/Shooting Star. 76-77: Bob Fitch/Black Star. 101: Courtesy of Kurusa. 106: David Parker/Science Photo Library/Photo Researchers. **Glossary:** G0: Stephen Wilkes/The Image Bank; Superstock; Bob Croxford/The Stock Market. G1: James Carmichael/The Image Bank; Bob Burch/Bruce Coleman; Rod Planck/Photo Researchers. G2: John M. Roberts/The Stock Market. G5: R.T. Cochran/Superstock. G6: Jeff Gnass/The Stock Market. G9: Fletcher & Baylis/Photo Researchers. G12: Comstock. G14: Four By Five, Inc.

ACKNOWLEDGMENTS

The publisher gratefully acknowledges permission to reprint the following copyrighted material:

"All the Ones They Call Lowly" by David Campbell from A CARIBBEAN DOZEN. Edited by John Agard & Grace Nichols. Illustrations © 1994 Cathie Felstead. Permission granted by Walker Books Limited, London. Published in the U.S. by Candlewick Press, Cambridge, MA.

"And my heart soars" by Chief Dan George. Copyright © 1974 by Chief Dan George and Helmut Hirnschall. Reprinted by permission of Hancock House Publishing Ltd. 19313 Zeroz Ave., Surrey, BC V3S 5J9, Canada.

Illustration from BEAT THE STORY DRUM, PUM-PUM retold and illustrated by Ashley Bryan. Copyright © 1980 Ashley Bryan. Reprinted with permission of Atheneum Books for Young Readers, an imprint of Simon & Schuster Children's Publishing Division.

"Cactus Hotel" from CACTUS HOTEL text by Brenda Z. Guiberson, illustrated by Megan Lloyd. Text copyright © 1991 by Brenda Guiberson. Illustrations copyright © 1991 by Megan Lloyd. Reprinted by permission of Henry Holt and Co.

"Cloudy With a Chance of Meatballs" is from CLOUDY WITH A CHANCE OF MEATBALLS by Judi Barrett. Copyright © 1978 by Judi Barrett, illustrations copyright © 1978 by Ron Barrett. Reprinted with permission from Atheneum Books for Young Readers, an imprint of Simon & Schuster Children's Publishing Division.

Illustration from THE DANCING GRANNY retold and illustrated by Ashley Bryan. Copyright © 1977 by Ashley Bryan. Reprinted with permission of Atheneum Books for Young Readers, an imprint of Simon & Schuster Children's Publishing Division.

"Dream Wolf" is from DREAM WOLF by Paul Goble. Copyright © 1990 by Paul Goble. Reprinted with the permission of Simon & Schuster Books For Young Readers.

"A Fruit & Vegetable Man" from A FRUIT & VEGETABLE MAN by Roni Schotter. Text Copyright © 1993 by Roni Schotter; Illustrations copyright © 1993 by Jeanette Winter. By permission of Little, Brown and Company.

Cover permission for THE GIRL WHO LOVED WILD HORSES by Paul Goble. Copyright 1978 by Paul Goble. Reprinted with the permission of Simon & Schuster Books For Young Readers.

"Gone" from ONE AT A TIME by David McCord. Copyright © 1970 by David McCord. By permission of Little, Brown and Company.

"The Great Kapok Tree" from THE GREAT KAPOK TREE: A TALE OF THE AMAZON RAIN FOREST, copyright © 1990 by Lynne Cherry, reprinted by permission of Harcourt Brace & Company.

"An Incredible Journey" Water cycle board game adapted from "An Incredible Journey" in the Project Wet Curriculum and Activity Guide a publication of Project WET. Illustration by Peter Grosshauer.

"In Memory" by Ericka Northrop from JACK AND JILL, copyright © 1989 by Children's Better Health Institute, Benjamin Franklin Literary & Medical Society, Inc., Indianapolis, Indiana. Used by permission.

"In Time of Silver Rain" from SELECTED POEMS by Langston Hughes. Copyright © 1938 and renewed 1966 by Langston Hughes. Reprinted by permission of Alfred A. Knopf Inc.

Cover permission for ISLAND BOY by Barbara Cooney. Copyright © 1988 by Barbara Cooney Porter. Used by permission by Viking Penguin, a division of Penguin Books, USA Inc.

Illustration from LION AND THE OSTRICH CHICKS retold and illustrated by Ashley Bryan. Copyright © 1986 Ashley Bryan. Reprinted with permission of Atheneum Books for Young Readers, an imprint of Simon & Schuster Children's Publishing Division.

"Miss Rumphius" from MISS RUMPHIUS by Barbara Cooney. Copyright © 1982 by Barbara Cooney Porter. Used by permission of Viking Penguin, a division of Penguin Books USA, Inc.

"Operation Rescue: Saving Sea Life from Oil Spills" by Christina Wilsdon. Copyright 1990 Children's Television Workshop (New York, New York). All rights reserved.

Cover permission for OX-CART MAN by Donald Hall, illustrated by Barbara Cooney. Copyright © 1979 by Barbara Cooney Porter for illustrations. Used by permission of Viking Penguin, a division of Penguin Books USA Inc.

"Preserven el Parque Elysian" by Mike Kellin. Copyright © 1965 (renewed) by APPLESEED MUSIC INC. All Rights Reserved. Used by Permission.

"Que llueva!"/"It's Raining" from ARROZ CON LECHE by Lulu Delacre. Copyright © 1989 by Lulu Delacre. English lyrics by Elena Paz. Reprinted by permission of Scholastic, Inc.

"Rain Forests Around the World" from WHY SAVE THE RAIN FOREST. Text © 1993 by Donald Silver. Illustrations © 1993 by Patricia Wynne. Silver Burdett Press, Simon & Schuster Elementary Group. Used by permission.

"The Rains in Little Dribbles" from SOMETHING BIG HAS BEEN HERE by Jack Prelutsky. Copyright © 1990 by Jack Prelutsky. Published by Greenwillow Books. Reprinted by permission.

"The Rooster Who Understood Japanese" is from THE ROOSTER WHO UNDERSTOOD JAPANESE by Yoshiko Uchida. Text copyright © 1976 by Yoshiko Uchida. Reprinted courtesy of the Bancroft Library University of California, Berkeley.

"Spring Rain" is from RHYMES ABOUT US by Marchette Chute. Published 1974 by E.P. Dutton. Copyright © 1974 by Marchette Chute. Reprinted by permission of Elizabeth Roach.

"Storm in the Night" is from STORM IN THE NIGHT by Mary Stolz. Text copyright © 1988 by Mary Stolz. Illustrations copyright © 1988 by Pat Cummings. Reprinted by permission of HarperCollins Publishers.

"The Streets Are Free" is from THE STREETS ARE FREE/LA CALLE ES LIBRE by Kurusa, translation Karen Englander. Copyright © 1981 by Ediciones Ekare-Banco del Libro, Caracas, Venezuela. Used by permission of the publisher.

"The Toad" from SPEAKING OF COWS AND OTHER POEMS by Kaye Starbird. Copyright © 1960, © renewed 1988 by Kaye Starbird, Reprinted by permission of Marian Reiner for the author.

"Tornado Alert" Entire text of TORNADO ALERT by Franklyn M. Branley. Text copyright © 1988 by Franklyn M. Branley. Reprinted by permission of HarperCollins Publishers.

"Turtle Knows Your Name" is from TURTLE KNOWS YOUR NAME by Ashley Bryan. Copyright © 1989 by Ashley Bryan. Reprinted by permission of Atheneum Books for Young Readers, an imprint of Simon & Schuster Children's Publishing Division.

"Valentine for Earth" from THE LITTLE NATURALIST by Frances Frost. Copyright © 1959 by Frances Frost. Published by McGraw-Hill. Reprinted by permission.

"Volcanoes" by Judith E. Rand from NATIONAL GEOGRAPHIC WORLD, February 1995. Copyright © 1995 by National Geographic Society.

"Weather Is Full of the Nicest Sounds" from I LIKE WEATHER by Aileen Fisher. Text copyright © 1963 by Aileen Fisher. Reprinted by permission of HarperCollins Publisher.

"Weather Report" by Jane Yolen reprinted by permission of Curtis Brown Ltd. Copyright © 1992 by Jane Yolen. First appeared in WEATHER REPORT. Published by Boyds Mills Press.

"The Wolves of Winter" by Rachel Bucholz, photographs by Jim Brandenburg, from BOY'S LIFE, February 1995. Copyright © 1995 by Boy Scouts of America. Reprinted by permission.

READING RESOURCES

Diagrams: From WEATHER FORECASTING by Gail Gibbons, copyright © 1987 by Gail Gibbons. Reprinted by permission of Four Winds Press, an imprint of Simon & Schuster Books For Young Readers.

Maps: "Indian Groups of North America" from UNITED STATES AND ITS NEIGHBORS, copyright © 1991 by Macmillan/McGraw-Hill School Publishing Company. Reprinted by permission of Macmillan/McGraw-Hill School Publishing Company.

Schedules: Excerpt from CalTrain Peninsula Rail Service timetable. Reprinted by permission of the California Department of Transportation.

COVER DESIGN: Carbone Smolan Associates
COVER ILLUSTRATION: Marc Mongeau

DESIGN CREDITS
Carbone Smolan Associates, front matter, 10-11
Bill Smith Studio, 72-73
Function Thru Form, Inc., 106-110
Notovitz Design Inc., 104-105, 111

ILLUSTRATION CREDITS
Marc Mongeau, 10-11; Susan Huls, 12-13, 29 (borders); Claudia Karabaic Sargent, 32, 34-38, 40-46 (borders); Kathy Jeffers, 48-49 (valentine globe); Grace De Vito, 72-73 (title panel); Leo Kubinyi, 72-73 (map); Steven Bennett, 74 (calligraphy); Jose Ortega, 102-103. **Reading Resources:** Brad Hamann, 104; Maria Lauricella, 106; Steve Sullivan, 107; Bob Mansfield, 108-109. **Glossary:** Lori Anzalone, G3, G4, G7, G8, G10, G13; Greg King, G15.

PHOTOGRAPHY CREDITS
All photographs are by the Macmillan/McGraw-Hill School Division (MMSD) except as noted below.

29: b. Jeannette Winter. 30: m.l. Courtesy of Nathaniel Gallardo. 30-31: m., b.r. Ken Kerbs for MMSD. 46: t. Douglas Merriam. 71: Courtesy Lynne Cherry . 74-75: Ken Straiton/Image Finders. 75: Yorham Kahana/Shooting Star. 76-77: Bob Fitch/Black Star. 101: Courtesy of Kurusa. 106: David Parker/Science Photo Library/Photo Researchers. **Glossary:** G0: Stephen Wilkes/The Image Bank; Superstock; Bob Croxford/The Stock Market; Bob Burch/Bruce Coleman; Rod Planck/Photo Researchers. G2: John M. Roberts/The Stock Market. G5: R.T. Cochran/Superstock. G6: Jeff Gnass/The Stock Market. G9: Fletcher & Baylis/Photo Researchers. G12: Comstock. G14: Four By Five, Inc.